KATHARINA SCHLEGL-KOFLER

Labrador Retrievers

Labrador Retrievers

KATHARINA SCHLEGL-KOFLER

CONTENTS

INFECTED BY LABRADORS

Even when I was a child, I loved dogs. In the late 1970s, I was finally able to persuade my parents to let me have one. A newspaper ad led us to a dog seller in the area. We really wanted a Dalmatian, but there were none available, so the man said we should take a Labrador. A what? That meant absolutely nothing to us. But of course the cuddly yellow puppy from England, Golden Sun of Kenstaff, moved in with us. Through the only book on retrievers available at the time, I stumbled onto the still-young National Retriever Club and became a member in 1977. I had been bitten by the Labrador bug. Later on another Lab came along, but from a better line of breeding, and in 1989 a yellow male moved in, Sir Dusty of Rembo's Junior's. Work with a training dummy eventually followed, and hunting trials were part of the program. I was an avowed yellow Lab fan, and in 2002 my yellow female, Beaverlodge's Brenda, came into my life. Work is her passion, and I entered her in working tests and hunting trials. In addition, she has been a mother many times and a grandmother. It's a sure thing that the next dog will also be a yellow Labrador!

Katharina Schlegl-Kofler

KATHARINA SCHLEGL-KOFLER has been involved with dogs for more than thirty years. In this time, she has always had a yellow Labrador. In the 1980's and 1990's she organized various shows. In 2005 and 2008 she bred two litters under the kennel name of Manyoaks. She is the author of numerous dog books and has operated a dog-training school for many years.

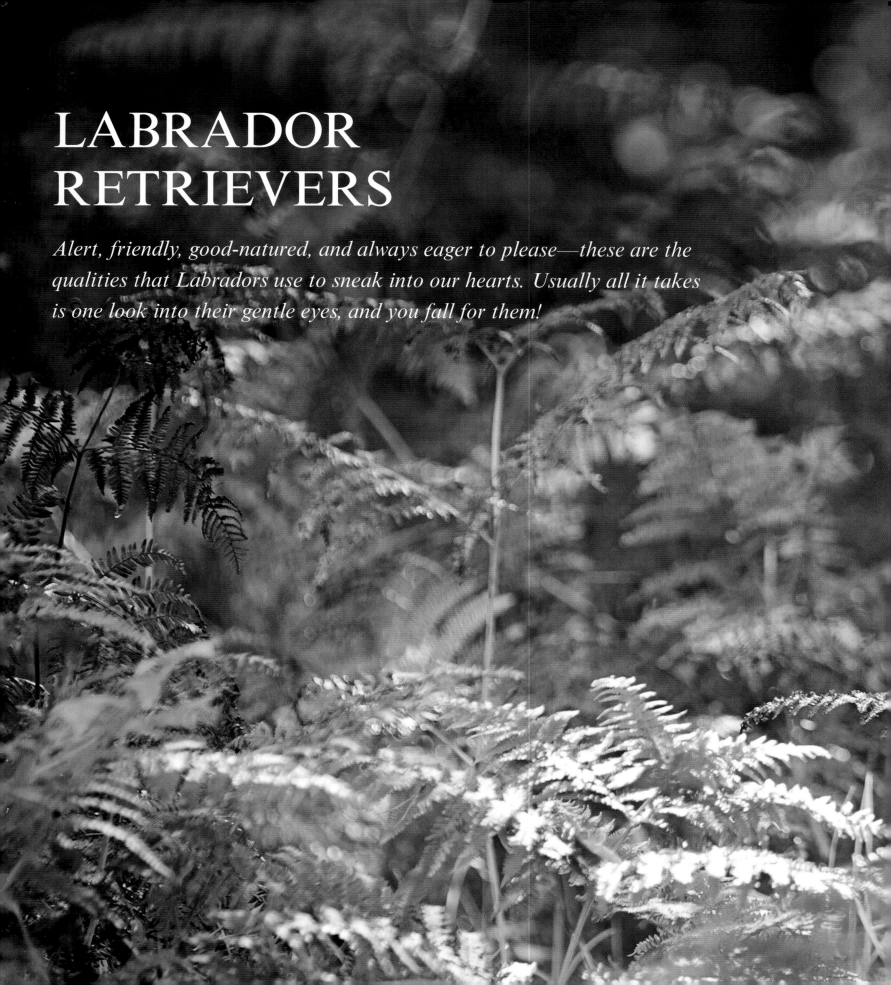

LABRADOR RETRIEVERS

Alert, friendly, good-natured, and always eager to please—these are the qualities that Labradors use to sneak into our hearts. Usually all it takes is one look into their gentle eyes, and you fall for them!

History

Anyone who likes to go for walks and who has an eye for dogs has known this for a long time: Whether yellow, brown, or black, there are Labs everywhere! With their straightforward nature, their always happy and friendly disposition, their faithfulness, and their devotion to humans, they began their victory march around the world from Great Britain. In this country, the Labrador now enjoys a permanent place among the five favorite dog breeds, and this applies to other countries as well. All the qualities that their fans love have their origin in the dogs' hunting abilities, where it is important for them to work with their owners. The Labrador has always been a hunting dog whose task is to quickly and reliably locate and fetch wild game, such as ducks, pheasants, and rabbits that have been brought down. The Labrador may retrieve for anyone in the hunting party, but will always prefer to bring the game to his owner.

How It All Began

The history of the Labrador Retriever began on the Canadian island of Newfoundland, offshore from the province of Labrador. Because of the harsh climate there, life was not easy for humans and animals. People needed sturdy dogs that were not sensitive to the weather and did not shrink from work in icy waters. These were the ancestors of the Labrador Retriever.

Arthur Holland-Hibbert, the 3rd Lord Knutsford (1855–1935), was very successful with his Labradors in both field trials and shows. Many of today's Labs from working lines still have the same physical appearance.

The first European to reach Newfoundland was John Cabot, who in 1497 was searching for a route from Europe to Asia. Because the waters were rich with fish, the island soon became a favorite destination for seafaring nations. The English developed a significant fishing industry there. But abundant fishing was not the only attraction, for the hunting was also excellent. Through the brisk flow of trade, various dog breeds, such as the St. Hubert Hound (a type of bloodhound) and dogs similar to Brackens and mastiffs, ended up on the island. Water dogs were most highly prized. Sturdy dogs that were not sensitive to the weather and loved the water, with a shaggy to curly coat, were used for more

than hunting. They also helped fishermen haul in the nets, retrieved fish that fell out of the nets, and even fetched pieces of equipment accidentally dropped overboard.

Initial Deliberate Breeding

Gradually, specific characteristics and visual traits became firmly established through deliberate breeding. Two types arose, both of which were originally called Newfoundland Dogs. One was fairly large and powerful with a coarse coat. It was used primarily for pulling loads and as a rescue dog in the recovery of shipwrecks.

The duty of the smaller Newfoundland Dog, which was also called the St. John's Dog, was hunting. It was usually black, but also yellow or red, shorthaired, and smaller than its large relative. The St. John's Dog was also faster and more agile, which, along with its exceptional nose, made it a highly esteemed hunting partner on land and in the water. It would retrieve tirelessly, and it worked well in all types of terrain and cold water. It took great satisfaction in retrieving and had a soft mouth, carrying wild game carefully without damaging it. According to old records there was also a longhaired version called the Wavy Coated Retriever. This type of dog was ill suited to fishermen: Ice built up in the long coat and brought lots of water into the boat.

Based on current knowledge, the St. John's Dog was the ancestor of the Labrador. This dog

The history of the Labrador Retriever began in Newfoundland; pure breeding originated in Great Britain. From there, the Lab found numerous devotees in many lands during the latter part of the twentieth century.

and the larger, longhaired type were described for the first time in 1814 by the devoted hunter Colonel Peter Hawker in his book *Instructions to Young Sportsmen*. He was enthusiastic about this dog's hunting abilities and the ease with which it could be trained. Precisely when and with whom the first St. John's Dogs reached England at this time is not known. But in the course of the nineteenth century, fewer of them were brought to England, because the commerce between England and Newfoundland declined. In addition, the quarantine law in Great Britain, which took effect in 1895, made it very difficult to import dogs.

These developments contributed to a scarcity of Labs for breeding. But, at the same time, the demand for retrievers for hunting increased, because developments in firearms made it possible to bag more wild game, especially birds. Thus, hunters found it necessary to create hybrids using other breeds with similar characteristics.

We can no longer reconstruct completely which breeds these were. According to old accounts, they included water spaniels and, presumably, pointers.

Pioneers in Breeding Labrador Retrievers

The breeding of Labrador Retrievers lay almost exclusively in the hands of the nobility because they owned the largest hunting estates. One of the main pioneers was the 2nd Earl of Malmesbury (1778–1841). Under the kennel name

Ch. Banchory Sunspeck (left, born 1917) from the kennel of Lorna, Countess Howe, and daughter Beaulieu Nance (right, born 1921) were good working dogs that were close to to the breed standard.

The dog's full name is *Labrador Retriever*, which refers to its original purpose. Carrying and retrieving come naturally to Labs.

Malmesbury, he and his descendants devoted nearly a century to developing a pure breed. The conditions for that endeavor were good, because the earl had imported many St. John's Dogs over time. Influential dogs from that breeding included Malmesbury Tramp (born 1878) and Malmesbury Sweep (born 1877), both of which produced many offspring. The Malmesburys first called their breed Labrador in 1887. Breeding by the Buccleuch family in Scotland was just as significant; their kennel of the same name still exists today. The founder was the 5th Duke of Buccleuch in 1835, along with his brothers Lord John Scott and Lord Home, who lived near them. They too had imported St. John's Dogs from Newfoundland and had acquired a few breeding dogs from the Malmesburys.

Around 1884, Arthur Holland-Hibbert (1855–1935), the later 3rd Viscount Knutsford, began breeding dogs descended from these lines, using the kennel name Munden. He was a founding member and director for many years of the English Labrador Retriever Club. His female Munden Single was the first to take part in a field trial. His male Munden Sentry was successful in shows. Both dogs were descendants of the Malmesbury studs.

Another founding member and director of the English Labrador Retriever Club, and an influential breeder, was Lorna, Countess Howe, with her kennel Banchory.

Breeding Goals

The breeding goals were exclusively to produce Labradors suited for hunting, and the retention of the qualities required for hunting. These were—and still are—an exceptional sense of smell, endurance, ruggedness in the face of severe weather as well as difficult terrain, and an enjoyment of the water. In addition, people valued the dogs' friendly nature and their trainability, combined with their desire to retrieve for their handlers.

Physical characteristics also distinguish a breed. With the Labrador, they were oriented toward hunting: The dog had to be neither too large nor too small, and had to be able to withstand strenuous days of hunting. A powerful build helped the Lab get through even difficult terrain. The dog also had to be able to jump easily over fences and walls with downed game in its mouth.

In 1887, the first official breed standard was compiled so that all these characteristics would be borne in mind as consistently as possible in breeding. In 1904, the Labrador Retriever was recognized as a breed by the Kennel Club, the British umbrella association for dog breeding. In 1916, the English Labrador Retriever Club was founded.

Field Trials

For successful breeding, it is essential to verify that a dog meets all the requirements (see pp. 52–59). Field trials (F.T. for short) were held as early as the end of the nineteenth century to evaluate hunting performance. During a hunt, the work of individual dogs was evaluated by judges. Previously, field trials were primarily for pointers, setters, and spaniels, and now retrievers were added. At first, mainly Flat Coated Retrievers were seen. In 1904, the first Labrador, Munden Single, entered a field trial and impressed everyone who saw it perform. In 1907, the three Labradors that took part in an important field trial captured the top three places. The winner was the male Flapper, who was descended from the Munden line. He was a distinguished stud dog and a field trial champion. The popularity of Labradors rose quickly, and many F.T. champions followed, including some very famous ones such as Peter of Faskally, Scandal of Glynn, Banchory Bolo, Banchory Sunspeck, and Titus of Whitmore.

Shows

Dog shows were held in England starting in the middle of the nineteenth century in order to examine the conformation (the appearance) of purebred dogs. The first such show took place in 1859 in Newcastle upon Tyne. In 1886, Charles Cruft started a show in Birmingham that has been known since 1891 as the Cruft Greatest Dog Show, or Crufts for short; even today it is the most important show in Great Britain, and it is considered the largest dog show in the world. Now even Labrador breeders began showing their dogs at shows.

The Dual-Purpose Labrador

In breeding Labrador Retrievers, performance and endurance were very closely linked, for both qualities were important to the effectiveness as a retriever in hunting. The goal was to produce a dual-purpose Labrador—a dog that could place high in both field trials and the show ring. A dog that won the championship in field trials and shows was known as a dual champion. Only ten Labradors have earned that title in Great Britain to this day. But this is not surprising, because it is no simple matter to become a champion of "just" a field trial or a show.

There were many Labradors that really didn't have what it took to win a championship, but were still very good in both areas. Among others, Lorna, Countess Howe, with her Banchory kennel, and the 3rd Lord Knutsford with Munden, were very committed to this type of dog. Lorna, Countess Howe's kennel alone produced four dual champions—Banchory Bolo (born 1915), Banchory Sunspeck (born 1917), Banchory Painter (born 1930), and Bramshaw Bob (born 1929); she had not bred them, but she owned them. The last dual champion was Knaith Banjo (born 1946), a large male dog belonging to Veronica Wormald. There were other dual-purpose Labradors in the 1960s and 1970s. One very famous male dog was F.T.Ch. Holdgate Willie (born 1969), who won his class at Crufts in 1974. Susan Scales, a famous breeder, who also used him as a stud,

In a hunt, small game, such as rabbits, ducks, and pheasants, was flushed by flushing dogs. Then the hunters shot it. In field trials, the handler and the leashed dog stand next to each other and must carefully observe what happens. Then the judges decide which dog is to fetch which game animal.

Even though Labradors are not always trained for hunting, they still are hunting dogs, and they are considered specialists for retrieving all downed game.

bred dogs at her kennel Manymills from 1960 until her death in 2000. Many of her dogs were successful in field trials and shows. One of them was Holdgate Willie. He won a field trial and took first place at shows several times. One of his sons, Abbeystead Heron's Court (born 1985), bred by Lynn Minchella, was a show champion, but also placed well in field trials. His name appears in many pedigrees, and he was a typical dual-purpose Labrador.

Labrador Retrievers in North America
Since 1991, the Lab has been the most popular dog breed in North America, but it got off to a rather slow start. The first Labrador Retriever was registered with the American Kennel Club in 1917, but by 1927 the Lab's numbers had climbed only to twenty-three. An article in a 1928 *AKC Gazette* titled "Meet the Labrador Retriever" sparked some new interest in this breed.

In 1929, Kinclaven Lowesby became the first registered yellow Lab in the United States.

(Originally the color was designated as *golden*.) The Labrador Retriever Club was founded in the United States in 1931, and in that year the first American field trial for Labs was held at Glenmere Court Estate in Chester, New York. The year 1932 saw the first registration of a liver-colored Lab—Diver of Chiltonfoliat—by the AKC. In 1933, a Lab named Ming was born in England; after coming to the United States it became the first yellow American field champion.

In 1938, *Life* magazine featured a dog on its cover: Blind of Arden, a black Lab owned by Averell Harriman. The dog became the top US retriever. In 1940 the first American-bred chocolate Lab was registered by the AKC as Kennoway's Fudge. The National Retriever Club was established in the United States in 1941. In the years after World War II, the popularity of the Labrador gained momentum.

During the Vietnam War era, some Labrador Retrievers were deployed as American war dogs. They were trained at the British Jungle Warfare

School in Malaysia. The United States military considered war dogs expendable equipment, and very few of them were allowed to return home after their service. Most American war dogs were German Shepherds, but Labrador Retrievers were used by the navy to detect underwater divers. Labs were also used for tracking, for locating wounded soldiers and downed airmen, and for detecting enemy patrols. Six Labs were killed in action in Vietnam. President Bill Clinton owned two Labs—Buddy and Seamus. As president, he signed a bill allowing the adoption of retired military dogs by civilians.

In 1991, Storm's Riptide Star was born. This dog was the first chocolate Lab to win the American national field championship (1996).

In the United States, Labrador Retrievers are popular hunting dogs, but most are family pets. In the field, they are often used as flushing dogs for upland game and as retrievers for downed waterfowl. They can also be trained to point. In the United States, there are twice as many Labrador Retrievers as there are the second-most popular dog.

Labs are the most highly esteemed assistance dogs; 60–70 percent of all guide dogs in the United States are Labs. The Labradoodle was bred to produce a dog with the disposition of a Labrador and the hypoallergenic coat of a poodle. (The second desired effect is not universally achieved.) Although Labrador Retrievers are excellent for companionship, assistance, hunt-

ing, and guiding, their outgoing, friendly nature makes them only mediocre guard dogs.

Some Labradors tend to gluttony, so they need a controlled diet and regular exercise, including at least two half-hour walks a day. It is estimated that in the United States 25 percent of dogs are overweight, which can induce problems in the knees and hips. Labs will play fetch with a ball or dummy for hours, but they must avoid overheating in summer weather. They are passionate water dogs, and their swimming is enhanced by webbed toes. This feature also keeps winter's snow and ice from accumulating between the toes.

In 1996, the National Labrador Retriever Club was founded. It recognizes the breed standard set by the Fédération Cynologique Internationale (FCI), and it offers a breeders directory, a *Guide to Buying a Labrador*, and a newsletter for members, *The Labrador Connection*.

The Labrador Retriever in Other Countries

Besides the United States, Great Britain is "Labrador land." According to the English Kennel Club, more than 44,000 Lab puppies were born in Great Britain in 2010. (Three times as many are registered in the United States every year.) Labs are also number one in Canada and the Netherlands. The Scandinavian countries and France are also at the forefront of Lab ownership.

The Lab's appearance has evolved over time. These specimens embody today's show type. This type is particularly popular among dog show aficionados.

The Other Retriever Breeds

The Labrador is the most common, but not the only, breed of retriever. There are five more retriever breeds. Four of them are closely related to the Labrador.

NOVA SCOTIA DUCK TOLLING RETRIEVER

A dog that originated in Canada, presumably from Koojkerhondjes, spaniels, and Shelties, it is used to lure ducks within shooting range (that is, duck tolling) with its playful behavior on the shore. When the ducks are shot, the dog's job is to retrieve them. The Toller is a distant relative of the other retrievers. It is playful and happy, but can also be stubborn, so persistence and firmness are important in training. The dog has a guarding instinct and is rather indifferent toward strangers.

LABRADOR RETRIEVER

The ancestor of the Labrador is the St. John's Dog. This dog played an essential role in the appearance of the four other retriever breeds, and the common origin is recognizable despite the different appearances.

CURLY COATED RETRIEVER

Also known as the Curly, this oldest retriever breed originated in Great Britain, where it is quite rare. Its characteristic curly coat is a legacy from the water dogs. Its ancestors include the St. John's Dog, but its other forebears remain unknown. The Curly is black or liver colored; originally there was also a yellow line, but the color did not gain acceptance, and nowadays it is not allowed. Curlies are late-maturing, happy dogs that sometimes have a hard head and show an instinct for guarding and protecting.

CHESAPEAKE BAY RETRIEVER

Its home is the bay of the same name in the eastern United States. Its ancestors were probably a red and a black St. John's Dog that were further crossed with Curlies, Flats, water spaniels, and setters. This tough retriever breed works even under the most extreme weather conditions and even when other retrievers give up. Chessies are happy, slow to mature, and fairly reserved with strangers, and they show an instinct for guarding and watching. They come in several shades of brown.

FLAT COATED RETRIEVER

The Flat, another British breed, came from the black Irish Setters of the time that were crossed with St. John's Dogs and Collie-type dogs. In the nineteenth century, it was the best-known retriever. The Flat is friendly and likes to learn. It is quite lively but rather temperamental, and in training this requires patience, calm, and consistency. Flat Coated Retrievers are black or liver colored. Sometimes there are yellow examples, but in Flats yellow is not an allowable color.

GOLDEN RETRIEVER

Its ancestors were yellow Wavy Coated Retrievers, probably the longhaired variants of the St. John's Dog. They too were brought into England by the nobility, and were crossed with liver-colored Tweed Water Spaniels, black retrievers, and a sandy-colored bloodhound. Then they were bred only with yellow, longhaired dogs. The golden is gentle and outgoing. Before the advent of the Labrador, it was the number-one fashionable dog, which is not good for any breed.

The Breed Today

For a long time the Labrador was exclusively a hunting dog for the rich, but that changed around the middle of the twentieth century, and it found a growing number of devotees outside the nobility in its homeland. This was because the standard of living improved, and even "normal" people could afford to own purebred dogs and to go hunting. But the Labrador won friends outside the hunting circle, too. Its friendly and down-to-earth nature, its trainability, and its will to please by forming a close bond with its handler turned the Labrador into an increasingly popular, pure companion dog, even for nonhunters. The dog was also well suited to other areas. Because of its pleasant and intelligent nature, it performs well as a guide dog and as an escort for people with disabilities.

The Divergence of the Breeds

Not everyone who learned about Labradors was interested in hunting.
Many enjoyed dog shows, and others simply wanted a family dog.

Despite the divergent development of the lines, hunting skills are still important to some show-line breeders.

Labrador fans who had no connection to hunting began breeding dogs. In Great Britain, starting in the 1930s, the breed began to diverge slowly but surely into *show lines* (sometimes also called *standard lines*) on the one hand, and working lines (sometimes also referred to as *field trial lines*), on the other. Many critical voices warned against splitting the breed and allowing the working qualities to fade into the background. In order to prevent dogs without breed-specific working qualities from becoming show champions, the awarding of this title was temporarily tied to passing a working test. The Labradors had to show that they were not gun-shy, retrieved game with a soft mouth, and were sufficiently useful in searching and retrieving.

From Working Line to Show Line

Despite all efforts to the contrary, the divergent development of the breed in two directions could not be halted. At shows, the dogs' appearance, detached from the intended purpose of hunting, stepped increasingly into the foreground, and in the working category, the level of performance rose steadily. There were more and more show judges who had no connection to hunting, and thus did not necessarily evaluate the dogs on the physical qualities required for strenuous days of hunting. Although the original breed standard changed only slightly in certain points, in 1950, and again in 1986, it was gradually construed differently. The show type changed more and more. Heavier dogs were increasingly awarded prizes in show rings. Anyone who wanted success in shows bred dogs in that direction. Famous kennel names since the 1980s include Poolstead, Charway, Kupros, Lawnwood, Fabracken, and Rocheby.

Dogs from working lines, on the one hand, showed up less frequently in the show ring, because their lighter physique meant they hardly had a chance of earning a favorable evaluation.

The change in appearance resulted from a different interpretation of the breed standard, although the exact wording remained practically unchanged. Here we see the head of a typical show line female (top) and a male.

At field trials, on the other hand, only dogs from working lines could cope with the requirements. Famous kennel names since the 1980s include Drakeshead, Pocklea, Swinbrook, Halstead, Birdbrook, and Blackharn.

This development made things difficult for dual-purpose Labradors. Dogs that could perform well at both field trials and shows were rare. Unfortunately, successful dual-purpose dogs were often largely ignored by breeders. F.T.Ch. Strathfieldsaye Calcot Strossbow (born 1970), descended mainly from show lines, was hardly used as a stud by breeders for either show lines or working lines. Despite his successful career at Crufts, F.T.Ch. Holdgate Willie was used almost exclusively by breeders of working lines. One of the last true dual-purpose Labradors was the grandson of the previously mentioned Holdgate Willie, Abbeystead Heron's Court (born 1985). There have not been any dual-purpose champions since Knaith Banjo (born 1946).

Nowadays, there are again critical voices among breeders and judges who remember the original breeding goals and feel that they should not be lost from view. In 2009, the British Kennel Club even expanded the breed standard with some observations intended to avoid any exaggerations that could have a negative effect on health and functionality. So, for example, the trend toward increasingly large, heavy dogs resulted in decreased resilience. At least on pa-

per, this is a small step back in the direction of "form follows function."

Developments in the United States

The split into show and working lines of course took place in other countries as well. Here too both camps exist, and there is always discussion about whether this is good or bad for the breed in the long run. But there are also lines that are not purely for show or for work. Many pedigrees contain both types to varying degrees.

Differences Between Show and Working Dogs

You may be wondering how there can be such a difference in a single standard, because a Labrador is a Labrador, right? Below you will see the differences that have resulted from different interpretations of the standard and from differing breeding goals.

Appearance

You will first notice the different appearance.
• Many dogs from working lines resemble the original Labrador type. They are powerful and muscular, but not massive; the head is lighter, and the stop, the transition from snout to forehead, is not so pronounced. Many lack the typical appearance of a Labrador. But a very diminutive Labrador, with a light frame and a pointed or long muzzle, also does not correspond to the earlier standard.

The will to please is one of the Labrador's most distinguishing traits. A Labrador with a will to please works closely with his owner and tries to do everything right.

• Dogs from show lines are stockier and have significantly more substance. The head is heavier and broader, and the muzzle is often relatively short. In comparison with many dogs from working lines, their legs are shorter. Not all dogs from show lines have the same physical build, however. There are bulkier specimens that would not be physically capable of withstanding strenuous days of hunting and working in trackless terrain, and even fewer fairly slender dogs that are truly agile.

Character

Aside from appearance, dogs from the two breeding lines differ in their character and personality traits.

• Labradors from working lines usually are very focused on their handlers. They are very friendly toward strangers, but sometimes less interested in them. They are eager to please and show a pronounced willingness to subordinate. They do not need outside motivation to cooperate; they are naturally willing because they have the above-mentioned will to please. They really enjoy working, tracking, and retrieving, and, in the field, they show great toughness and are not deterred from their work by adversity or thorny brush. Of course there are exceptions.

Because of their obedience, they are very sensitive and easily impressionable. In training, this requires good empathy and a proper appreciation of your Lab. Sometimes the Lab's sensitivity is too highly developed: The consequences are a certain degree of insecurity or mistrust of strangers and/or the people around the handler.

Despite the Lab's temperament and his quickness, he must be steady. In other words, he must have adequate inner calm to wait quietly and unexcitedly to be put into action, even in the presence of strong stimuli such as gunfire, water, and flying ducks or dummies. If the Lab has too much passion to work and/or if there is too little emphasis on calm during training, his steadiness will suffer. Undesirable characteristics such as whining, impatience, nervousness, and a hard mouth may be the result. Such Labs need calm, meticulous training.

• There is a broad spectrum of Labradors from show lines. Since the working qualities are not stressed in many of the breeding lines, there are all kinds of variants, from dogs with good working abilities to others that totally lack an interest in working and retrieving. Many of them are very temperamental, whereas others are decidedly composed and less active. Focus is generally less pronounced,

as is the will to subordinate. Many dogs from show lines behave more independently and have a will of their own. They usually are very secure with environmental stimuli, and they prove exceptionally friendly and outgoing with strangers. Because they are not as easy to impress and unnerve, training often requires more concentration on the part of the owner. For that reason, a Labrador from show lines is not so quick to find fault with mistakes by his handler. But of course there are exceptions to this too.

What About the Dual-Purpose Labrador?
There certainly are breeders who even today are committed to this original, versatile type. Few of them seek the goal of placing high in both categories, but rather try to avoid extremes in either breeding line and produce a Labrador with all the qualities inherent to the breed.

Compare a female from show lines (left) and one from working lines (who recently had a litter of puppies). The head and the physique of the Lab from working lines are lighter.

Appearance usually indicates whether Labradors such as these come from show or working lines. But ultimately what counts most are the ancestors in the pedigree.

Lines and Breeding Types

Show and working lines, breeding for hunting, or standard breeding—for most beginners with Labradors, these activities are initially very confusing. All these points apply to Labradors in many countries registered with the clubs associated with the Fédération Cynologique Internationale (FCI) and the American Kennel Club (AKC).

Show or Working Line?

How can we tell which line a Labrador comes from? It's not just the appearance or the behavior, because not every slightly built Labrador comes from working lines and not every less tractable representative of the breed is necessarily from show lines. In the final analysis, a look at the pedigree is the only source of reliable information about a dog's origin. One criterion is the kennel names of the ancestors, but to a beginner they mean nothing at first. However, certain titles in the pedigrees of the listed dogs provide clear indications. With dogs from show lines, there are often champion titles before the names of ancestors, such as these:

• Show Champion (Sh. Ch.)
• Junior Champion (Jr. Ch.)
• Champion (Ch.)
• National Champion
• Club Champion

If the dog comes from working lines, you will often find these additions to the ancestors' names:
• Field Trial Champion (F. T. Ch.)
• Field Trial Winner (F. T. Winner)
• Working Champion (W. Ch.)

If a Labrador has ancestors from both lines, you will find additions from both areas.

Breeding Types

The breeding types, in which one must distinguish between standard and hunting, are quite different. This has nothing to do with the lines, but tells something about whether the parents or grandparents have succeeded in any hunting trials, and which ones.
• "Standard breeding": One or both parents lack specific hunting trials. But the dogs can still be from working lines, or may have passed nonhunting trials such as in dummy sport. The sometimes common designation *standard line* for show lines has nothing to do with *standard breeding*. That's not so easy at first glance!
• Breeding for hunting: Both parents, regardless of their lines, must have passed at least one retrieving trial.
• Special breeding for hunting performance: In this case, not only the parents, but also all of the grandparents of a dog, regardless of their lines, must have passed appropriate hunting trials and at least one retrieving trial.

Lines and Breeding Types

While hunting, the Labrador must always wait calmly until after the handler has fired and signaled the retrieve. The Lab was not bred to flush or to chase game. This is why the dogs generally are more unruffled with game than many other hunting dog breeds, such as German Wirehairs and beagles.

But there is a certain range with respect to the expression of the hunting instinct, and it depends on neither the line nor the trials passed, but rather on the dog's individual disposition. There are many representatives of the breed whose "hunting mood" really is turned on in the context of a real hunting situation with the hunter, a shotgun, and all the rest, and outside this typical situation they remain totally serene in the presence of game. Then there are passionate hunters that scan the surroundings on every walk, and surprise their owner with sudden disobedience and an "away-I-go!" Sometimes there are also Labradors that have only a casual interest in game or none at all, but this is not common to the breed.

Breeding types only tell something about specific trials entered by their ancestors, but nothing about whether a Labrador is from show or working lines, or, like these three, a mixture of both.

My Story

In my childhood and adolescence, I experienced many dogs of various breeds in my immediate surroundings. But when I thought about a dog, I always thought about a Labrador Retriever. For me, a dog was a Labrador, and nothing else.

Ulrike Weber likes to attend shows with Jo and Paula, and she has had quite a lot of success with Jo. But she also loves keeping her dogs busy with activities specific to retrievers.

A trip to England in the early 1970s solidified these thoughts, for we kept meeting more Labrador Retrievers in the houses of our host families. It stuck in my memory how these dogs lived and moved, especially their relaxed, friendly nature and their keen enjoyment of life.

So, much later, when my family situation made it possible to think about getting a dog of my own, there was never any question about which breed it would be!

Our first yellow Labrador came from a rescue situation. Up to that point, this dog had practically lived on the sofa and had not seen much of its surroundings. He was poorly trained, spoiled, and overweight. With his previous owners, he kind of took care of himself. He was cared for, but the people didn't do anything with him. He could not form a bond with people; on the contrary, he had learned to fend for himself.

He was initially a bit overwhelmed with his new life, with plenty of exercise in our yard with horses and other animals. His self-reliance, in combination with his hunting dog genes, meant that he was always on sniffing expeditions in the neighborhood, and very frequently we had to pick him up or go looking for him.

When a female Labrador came to us not long afterward, I found out that things didn't have to be that way. From the beginning, I gave her lots of attention, and the things and exercises that we did together gave this young female so much

joy that she never left my side. With her, I really experienced how much these dogs enjoy learning, and how much they need to be challenged. She showed me how ready Labradors are to bond with people who give them direction and who have pleasant experiences with them and can provide them with little adventures in everyday life.

That was in the early 1990s, and ever since, we have always had Labrador Retrievers in my family. These wonderful, lovable dogs changed our lives in a way that we could not have imagined.

After these two very different experiences, we were again on the lookout for a puppy, and, in the meantime, it became clear that only a puppy from a serious FCI breeding line would qualify. It was a female that gave us thirteen years of pure joy as a family dog. She was always there, and loved to accompany us on long hikes, streak through the woods, jump out of a boat into the lake, and wait on the beach until someone would go in for a dip so she could swim along. In addition, with her friendly, gentle nature she has been able to win over people who formerly were afraid of dogs. Just like a Labrador!

We began new chapters with another female dog that came to us as a puppy: We discovered shows and breeding. She had some good successes at shows and her health was excellent, so I was able to achieve my long-cherished wish of starting a breeding kennel. So far we have raised three litters, and each time it has been an inde-

Labradors once and for all is Ulrike Weber's motto. She enjoys living with her dogs and would not want to do without them and all the things they do together.

ULRIKE WEBER has belonged to Labrador Retriever associations since 1997, both at home and abroad: the British Labrador Retriever Club, the Midland Counties Labrador Retriever Club, and the Labrador Club of Scotland. Under the name FairFriends Show Line Labradors, she has been a breeder since 2008. She works with her dogs and regularly attends shows. In addition, she has a hunting license, and since 2010 she has worked as a dog psychologist in training puppies and young dogs.

scribable experience to be surrounded by the little Lab puppies with their amazing charm.

Even my young dog has opened up new worlds for me, because, despite the fact that she is from show lines and has been very successful in shows, she is a good worker. Because of her I got a hunting license and have done some hunting trials with her.

I am excited about how my "dog story" will continue. We cannot imagine a life without our beloved Labrador Retrievers, and we are very thankful to be able to live with these wonderful dogs.

Ulrike Weber
FairFriends Labrador Retrievers

The FCI/AKC Standard

The mandatory breed standards of all recognized dog breeds, including the standard for Labradors, are housed with the world's largest umbrella organization for dogs, the Fédération Cynologique Internationale (FCI), headquartered in Belgium. The American Kennel Club (AKC) standard is very similar to the FCI standard; however, if you wish to show your Labrador in the United States, you should first consult the AKC Standards.

The breed standard in force today dates from 1987, and it was amended on January 20, 2012. In 1987, some stipulations regarding character were incorporated into the standard for the first time, and the specification about the *stop* was changed from the original *slight to distinct* (1950) to *clearly defined.*

The Labrador is part of the FCI Group 8 (Retrievers, Flushing Dogs, and Water Dogs).

The otter tail is a typical breed characteristic. It provides stability during such tasks as jumping over an obstacle while carrying a rabbit or retrieving a duck from water with a strong current.

GENERAL PHYSICAL APPEARANCE
Strongly built, short-coupled, very active (which excludes excess weight or corpulence); broad in skull; broad and deep in chest and ribs; broad and strong over loins and hindquarters.

BEHAVIOR/TEMPERAMENT (DISPOSITION)
Good-tempered, very agile. Excellent nose, soft mouth; keen lover of water. Adaptable, devoted companion. Intelligent, keen, and biddable, with a strong will to please. Kindly nature with no trace of aggression or undue shyness.

HEAD

CRANIAL REGION
Skull: Broad, clean-cut, without fleshy cheeks.
Stop: Defined.

FACIAL REGION
Nose: Wide, nostrils well developed.
Muzzle: Powerful, not pointed.
Jaw/Teeth: Jaw of medium length; jaws and teeth strong with a perfect, regular, and complete scissor bite, i.e., the upper teeth closely overlapping lower teeth and set square to the jaws.
Eyes: Medium size, expressing intelligence and good temper; brown or hazel.
Ears: Not large or heavy, hanging close to the head and set rather far back.

NECK
Clean, strong, powerful, set into well-placed shoulders.

BODY
Back: Level topline.
Loins: Wide, short-coupled, and strong.
Chest: Of good width and depth, with well-sprung barrel ribs. This impression must not be achieved through excess weight.

TAIL
Distinctive feature, very thick toward the base, gradually tapering to the tip, medium length without feathering, but clothed thickly all around with short, thick, dense coat thus giving rounded appearance described as otter tail. *Can be carried gaily, but should not curve over back.*

LIMBS
FOREQUARTERS
Forelegs well boned and straight from the elbow to the ground when viewed from either front or side.
Shoulders: Long and sloping.

HINDQUARTERS
Well developed, not sloping to tail.
Stifle: Well turned.
Hocks: Well let down, cow hocks highly undesirable.

FEET
Round, compact: well-arched toes and well-developed pads.

GAIT
Free, covering adequate ground, straight and true in front and rear.

COAT
Hair:
Distinctive feature, short, dense, without wave or feathering; giving fairly hard feel to the touch; weather-resistant undercoat.

Color:
Wholly black, yellow, or liver/chocolate. Yellows range from light cream to red fox red. Small white spot on chest permissible.

SIZE
Ideal height at withers: Males 22–22½ inches (56–57 cm), females 21.5–22 inches (54–56 cm).

FAULTS
Any departure from the foregoing points should be seen as flaws, and the seriousness with which the faults should be regarded should be in exact proportion to their degree.

Comments
Male animals must have two apparently normal testicles fully descended into the scrotum.

A typical Labrador head looks round overall. The top of the head is broad, and the muzzle is not too long and pointed. Dark eyes give the Lab a particularly gentle appearance.

Defined stop

Wide cranial region,
without fleshy cheeks

Powerful muzzle,
not pointed

Neck clean
and strong

Short, thick coat with
weather-resistant
undercoat

The Labrador at a Glance

Paws compact
and round

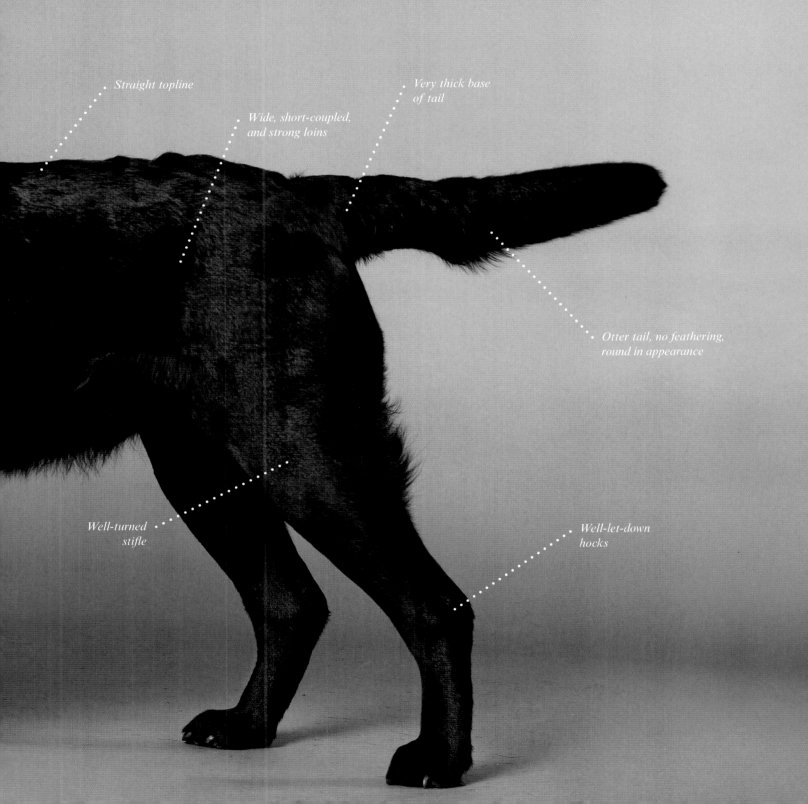

Straight topline

Wide, short-coupled, and strong loins

Very thick base of tail

Otter tail, no feathering, round in appearance

Well-turned stifle

Well-let-down hocks

33

Colors

On pages 18 and 19 you read about the Labrador's relatives: The colors black, yellow, and chocolate / liver / brown—and these alone—have occurred practically since the beginning of pedigreed breeding in all four British retriever breeds. It is considered certain that the predisposition for yellow and brown was "imported" from the St. John's Dogs. If there had been any other solid colors over the course of pedigreed breeding of Labradors in Great Britain, there would be appropriate evidence and photos in the literature.

Labradors are always one color, even when the parents are of different colors. Puppies in a litter do not always have the same color. Even litters with three colors are possible.

With Golden Retrievers yellow was selected for breeding early on; Flat-coated Retrievers were selected for black and liver colors; and likewise with Curly-coated Retrievers, only black and liver are permitted. With Labradors, all three colors and only these are approved. But the two other colors have always had their devotees. Nowadays the colors silver and charcoal occasionally turn up in Labradors outside the FCI, but they did not develop during pure breeding and therefore the FCI does not recognize them. They come primarily from the United States and presumably are the result of crossing with other breeds.

Black

With Labradors, black has always been by far the most common color, for it is passed on as a dominant trait. It is a deep, even black that makes the coat shine. Black is especially common in the working lines.

Yellow

The St. John's Dog initially came in other colors, but for a long time, only black Labradors were desired. In addition, yellow is passed on as a recessive trait, and thus it is less common.

In 1899, Maj. Charles Radclyff's Ben of Hyde was born—the first yellow Labrador to be officially registered in the Kennel Club. In 1915, Veronica Wormald founded her kennel Knaith, which was important to the breeding of yellow Labradors. Her male dog Knaith Banjo was very influential. He and Edgar Winter's equally significant stud Staindrop Saighdear (born 1944) were the only yellow dual champions.

In 1924, the Yellow Labrador Retriever Club was founded to promote the yellow Labrador; the chairman for many years, until his death, was Major Wormald, and he was followed by Veronica Wormald. Initially, there was even a separate standard in the FCI for yellow Labradors. But since all Labradors are descended from the same source, this standard was not recognized by the Kennel Club. The club still exists today with the same goals as when it was founded.

As you have already seen in the breed standard, yellows range from light cream to fox red. With yellow Labradors, the color is often not totally even, except with the very light and the truly fox red (rather than dark yellow) dogs.

The ears, the bridge of the nose, and the back of the hind legs usually are darker than the rest. The underwool is often noticeably lighter than the top layer of the coat. The pigment and the color in the pads of the feet, the flews, the nose, and around the eyes should be as dark as possible. Many yellow Labradors have a "seasonal nose" that is darker in the summer and lightens in the fall and winter. Certain color combinations can produce what's known as Dudleys—yellow dogs without

Because of the St. John's Dog, there were three colors—black, yellow, and brown—in all four British retriever breeds. But only with the Labrador were all three preserved through breeding and enshrined in the standard.

pigment. Nose, foot pads, flews, and so on are flesh- or liver-colored. They are not desirable. But usually it is not possible to predict the ultimate shade of yellow that puppies in a litter will have.

Brown

According to the standard, this color is called chocolate or liver. The darker the shade, the more desirable. The pigment should be liver colored, not pink. There probably also were brown Labradors before the end of the nineteenth century, but because of the necessary genetic combination that is required, brown Labs were less common than yellow ones. Individual brown Labradors were visible at field trials before World War I, but yellow Labs were more popular. Intentional breeding began only toward the end of the 1930s. The main groundbreakers were the Cookridge and Tibshelf kennels. The female Cookridge Tango (born 1961) was the first brown Labrador to become a champion through success at shows. Brown Labradors are almost exclusively from show lines. But in Great Britain, breeders are attempting to establish brown in the working lines as well.

More on Color Inheritance

With reference to color inheritance, let's take a brief, simple side trip into genetics. This will also help you understand the inheritance of diseases.

Every Labrador color has its devotees. But black, which is conditioned by heredity, is by far the most common.

In order to plan for colors in breeding—for example to avoid the so-called "Dudleys"—it is necessary to know what genetic information the dog carries. This can be revealed through the pedigree, in which the colors of five generations of ancestors can be seen, through the colors of the dog's offspring, or through a gene test. This makes it possible to determine which other colors the Lab can pass on, even though they are not visible in it.

Genes and Alleles

Two genes play a role in color inheritance in Labradors—B and E. Each of these two genes has two means of expression (alleles). The alleles of the B gene are "B" and "b." "B" allows black, but "b" does not, and produces brown. The E gene likewise has two alleles: "E" means "spread of dark color (black or brown) over the entire body"; "e" does not allow this spread (except in the foot pads, flews, and eyes), and thus signifies a light color, yellow. "B" is dominant over "b" and "E" over "e." Every Labrador carries the B- and the E-gene with two alleles each. A puppy receives from each parent both an allele of the B-gene and one from the E-gene.

A Labrador is black if it carries a "B" and an "E" in its color code. The other two alleles can be different:
• BBEE = homozygous black
• BBEe = black, but carrying yellow

• BbEE = black, but carrying brown
• BbEe = black, but carrying yellow and brown

So a Labrador is yellow only when it receives the "e" allele from both parents:
• BBee = homozygous yellow
• Bbee = yellow, but carrying brown ("b")
• bbee = yellow, but without pigment (Dudley).

For a brown coat, the necessary "B" information from both parents is also required. In addition, the dog must have an "E," which permits the distribution of dark color:
• bbEE = homozygous brown
• bbEe = brown, but also carrying yellow through "e"

A Special Combination

Because yellow and brown Labradors always need the genetic information for the coat color from both parents, there is a particular case if that is not passed on. If a brown Labrador that carries no yellow (bbEE) is mated with a yellow one that carries no brown (BBee), every puppy carries the color code BbEe. The entire litter is black. Once a Labrador carries the genetic information "B" (allowing the production of black) and "E" (distribution of dark color over the body), the coat is black. But all these puppies carry brown and yellow.

Color Faults

Because dogs of mixed colors were involved in the development of the Labrador, a color legacy occasionally crops up from those times. White spots directly over the foot pads at the back of the legs are relatively common. Even dual champion Banchory Bolo had them, so this color variant is called Bolo pads. White spots may also appear on the chest, the underside of the chin, and the lower abdomen. Even brindle (striped) and black and tan (reddish-brown markings over the eyes, on the chest, and on the legs with an otherwise black coat) can occasionally crop up. These color variants are passed on as recessive traits, so the dog must inherit the genetic information from both parents for them to become visible.

Other color variants may result from genetic defects. Thus, smaller or larger patches of black hair may occur on a yellow dog. Conversely, white hairs may occur in a black coat. All color defects and colors other than the ones described in the standard result in excluding the affected dogs from showing.

Brown and chocolate are synonyms. This color occurs almost exclusively in show lines, and less frequently than black and yellow. A very dark shade is preferred.

Whether you choose black, yellow, or brown, all Labradors exhibit cheerfulness and playfulness.

MY LABRADOR

Is a Labrador Retriever set to enrich your family? Good decision! There are a few points to ponder before a cuddly little puppy moves in, because taking on a four-legged family member needs careful planning. What do you expect from your Lab, what do you want to do with it, and where can you find the one that's appropriate for you? Take plenty of time to address these questions, because you and your family will be spending many years with your Labrador.

The Labrador Decision

The Labrador's friendly, well-balanced disposition makes it the ideal family dog. It is resilient, adapts very well to the human daily routine, and likes to be involved in everything. In addition, it is happy and quick to learn—including some things you wish it wouldn't—is easy to train, and is happy to be with its family. But a Lab is not a good choice for a watchdog. Many Labradors do bark when someone comes, but ultimately they are happy every time someone visits. An instinct for guarding and watching is not a desirable trait in a Labrador; these traits are not compatible with its task as a retriever in hunting situations. But in all the hymns of praise, the Labrador is no unassuming dog that simply tags along. It doesn't train itself, and it needs sufficient mental activity and exercise. When it has good experiences with children and its needs are taken into consideration, it is a good friend to them. But it's the parents who bear the main burden of training and going for walks. Small children should not lead a Labrador by themselves because of its size.

How and Where To Find the Right Dog

In choosing a Labrador, you have decided on a purebred dog, and of course you expect your dog to be as healthy as possible and her temperament to match everything that makes up a Labrador.

Strict control of breeding is the only way to assure the greatest probability of producing a typical, healthy Labrador. Don't buy from backyard breeders and dog dealers. Oftentimes, female dogs are used as breeding machines and kept under bad conditions.

Whether you are looking for a family dog or a companion for hunting, dummy exercises, or similar work, the characteristics appropriate to the breed don't just fall from the sky, but result only when they are considered in the breeding. Strict breeding prescriptions are necessary, along with broad knowledge on the part of the breeder about the breed and genetics. To foster the breed, it is also important to collect as much information as possible about the ancestors of the breeding dogs and their offspring and to apply it to the planning process. That is the only way to maximize the likelihood of producing a healthy, typical representative. So where do you find this type of dog? We need to take a little detour into the world of dog breeding.

FCI and AKC

The Fédération Cynologique Internationale (FCI) is headquartered in Belgium; it is the worldwide umbrella organization for recognized dog breeding associations. The FCI sets general provisions for breeding and for show and trial dogs. In each of its eighty-six member countries, there is a national umbrella organization. The United States is not a member country of the FCI, but it has numerous other associations, of which the American Kennel Club (AKC) is the best known. Affiliated with the latter are purebred dog breeding associations that sometimes focus on just one or two breeds and adhere to the strict regulations of the AKC. If you want to get your Labrador involved in dummy and hunting trials, working tests, or field trials, or to show her at the national and international shows of the AKC/FCI, your Lab must have the appropriate, recognized pedigree from the FCI, AKC, or other national dog association.

AKC, NLRC, and Other Organizations

The American Kennel Club traces its history to 1884, when representatives of existing dog enthusiast clubs met in Philadelphia to form a new umbrella organization. The AKC introduced its own gazette in 1888; it has now been published for more than a century and is one of the oldest dog periodicals in existence. A detailed history of the AKC is available online at *www.akc.org/about/history.cfm*. The AKC maintains a breed registry and specific breed standards; the criteria that apply to Labrador Retrievers can be found at *www.akc.org/breeds/labrador_retriever/index.cfm*.

The National Labrador Retriever Club was founded in 1996. It exists for the protection and the improvement of the breed. It maintains a code of ethics and a breeders' directory, and it publishes a newsletter. It adheres to the FCI Labrador Retriever standard that is used in eighty or more countries. The NLRC is a membership organization, and a portion of members' dues goes to breed-specific research.

In addition to the national and international organizations, there are many state, regional, and local Labrador Retriever clubs. An online search will lead you to many associations and breeders.

These and other associations exist to promote the breed. They establish standards for breeders: Dogs selected for breeding are required to meet high standards. For example, they must be x-rayed for hip and elbow dysplasia, and must be examined for certain genetic diseases no longer than twelve months before each breeding cycle. A gene test is sometimes required for certain diseases.

And that's not all. A temperament test checks for behavior in various situations, including stressful ones—for example, around shooting, to be certain that a dog is not gun-shy. There is an evaluation to determine if a Labrador meets the physical standard. If the dog fails to meet the breeding regulation in even one feature, she is not granted authorization for breeding.

The clubs also offer breed-specific training, dummy trials, working tests, and hunting trials, and they support health programs and much more. The information about breeding dogs is collected in a data bank and can be read on the home pages of many clubs. Puppies of good lineage are usually sold through club puppy lists rather than through newspaper ads.

Choosing a Puppy with a Click

If you visit the web sites of the major kennel clubs, such as the AKC, you will find some useful links. Near the top of the screen there is a menu bar with buttons for *puppies, dog owners, breeders, clubs and delegates,* and *dog shows and trials.* Drop-down menus appear when you click on any of the buttons, and you can navigate and find practically any desired information: available puppies, breeders, registration forms, and much more. To locate a breeder, for example, you click on *find a puppy* and then on *select a breed*; then you enter your postal code and the distance you are willing to travel, and the screen lists the recognized breeders who meet the criteria. The Breeder tab also leads to an online DNA resource center and online breeder classified ads. The Puppy tab produces a drop-down menu where you can get further information about finding and choosing a puppy, plus references to veterinarian services.

You can locate puppies through the web pages of the major kennel clubs. If you are looking for an older purebred Labrador, you can easily find online references to breed-specific rescue associations. Rescued adult dogs sometimes come with unknown baggage; on the other hand, they may save you the trouble of raising and training a puppy.

Which Dog, and for Whom?

Because the breed was split into show and working lines, you should think about your plans for the future before you get a dog. To get an overview of the different representatives of the breed, it's a good idea to take a look in person.

There are numerous trials available to hunting enthusiasts and their dogs. Trials for young dogs, for example, involve a series of skills ranging from retrieving to complete field trials. The top dogs can advance through the ranks and become field trial champions.

On the web sites of the various breeding associations, you can find all kinds of scheduled events. By navigating through the sites and clicking on the appropriate tabs, you are likely to find trials, training events, and shows in your area.

The following are some points to consider as you search for the right type of Labrador for you.

Pure Family Dog

Is your Labrador to be a simple everyday companion without special training? If so, the working qualities do not need to be a main criterion. But think about your daily routine and your leisure-time activities: Which is a better choice for your family, a fairly sedate dog or an active one? Very bulky dogs often have less endurance than show-line Labradors with a more moderate build. You can also see whether you prefer a fairly vigorous dog or a more tractable one. Labradors from working lines are well suited to being family dogs as long as you are dealing with a more sensitive dog and do more than just go for walks with her. Many Labradors are not given enough to do if they are not challenged to use their natural talents.

In addition, breeders who produce dogs from working lines understandably prefer to sell their puppies to people who will also work with the dogs. Every Labrador that lives in a perfectly normal daily routine should have the typical balanced disposition, ease of training, and resilience—regardless of whether she is "only" a family dog or also has another job.

For Hunting

If you are looking for a hunting dog, think about whether you need an independent, fairly "tough" dog for your hunting situation, or a tractable dog that needs more guidance. Make sure that the parents have participated in hunting trials and have been used for hunting. It's ideal if you get a chance to see at least one of the parent dogs or their offspring at work on a hunting course.

For Dummy Sport

Do you intend to participate in dummy sport, or are you at least considering it? In either case, you should be sure that at least one of the parents has taken part in working tests and that both of them show willingness and endurance in retrieving.

If you would also like to advance to higher classes, or even climb through the ranks later on, you should choose a Labrador from working lines whose relatives have already performed successfully. But if you would rather attend working tests for fun without striving to win laurels, you can find appropriate dogs in both the working and the show lines.

Labradors are very versatile. Still, before you buy one, you should carefully consider your plans for the dog and what you eventually hope to do with her.

For Other Types of Dog Training

For rescue work, you need a Labrador that is not too bulky. It must take to any terrain and search tirelessly and quickly, always remaining in close contact with her handler.

Labradors that are used in social services as therapy dogs must be very people oriented, calm, and steady in the presence of noises and visual stimuli from the surroundings. Appropriate dogs are available from both show and working lines.

Participating in Shows

Do you want to show your Labrador? Then the most important consideration is the dog's appearance. You will find an appropriate dog only in show lines. The breeder should have experience in shows.

If you long for a championship title, you will need to search among breeders whose own dogs and puppies have achieved this type of success.

Breeders and Expenses

As you have already seen, sanctioned breeders need to meet certain criteria to ply their trade. Once these requirements are met, they are off and running, and there are some very different considerations: Just what is the goal of breeding? What are the strengths and the weaknesses of the female, and on that basis, which of the males is the right match?

An unmistakable characteristic of pedigrees from certain retriever and Labrador clubs is, among others, the "sparrow dog," the emblem of the hunting dog association.

Understanding a Pedigree

The pedigree contains the abbreviations and the complete names of the relevant clubs. You may also find the emblem of the FCI, plus the full name: Fédération Cynologique Internationale. Another unmistakable characteristic of such pedigrees is the "sparrow dog," the logo of the hunting dog association.

What the Pedigree Says

Of course the first thing you see is the name and breed book number of your dog and the information about the breeder. The names of the dog's siblings are also entered. Then come the relatives, from the parents to the great-grandparents. Every dog has a variety of information included under the name, usually in the form of abbreviations. But what do these mysterious "hieroglyphics" mean? The paragraphs below explain the information on a pedigree, using the example of a Labrador.

Pedigrees are often structured similar to a family tree. The dog's name and information should be at the top of the document, including breed, registration number, color, and a brief physical description. The upper part of a pedigree is reserved for information about the dog's sire (father), such as the sire's name, registration number, and some further information. The sire's parents are also included in the top part of the pedigree. You may even notice that one dog's name occurs more than once: This is

known as line breeding, a technique that some breeders use to strengthen their lines.

The bottom part of a pedigree focuses on your dog's dam (mother). As you might expect, the information includes her name, registration number, and notes about the litter that produced your dog. The dam's parents and grandparents are also included on the lower half of the pedigree, with sires listed above dams.

Your dog's pedigree may include references to titles at shows and trials. These are based on merit and achievement. Abbreviations such as *Ch.* and *UD* stand for *"champion"* and *"utility dog,"* respectively.

A pedigree also contains information on the dog's health. It will specify that your dog has been tested for certain defects, such as hip and elbow dysplasia. Gene tests for some breed-specific faults may be reported: progressive retinal atrophy, centronuclear myopathy, and exercise-induced collapse. The three tests should indicate that the dog in question carries no gene for these diseases.

Choosing the Parent Dogs

Many breeders first inspect potential sires on-site to form the clearest possible picture and make a decision to drive, sometimes significant distances, to the selected sire for mating at the proper time. Someday the new dog family will appear in the litter basket, and then there will be eight very beautiful but trying weeks of waiting. Everything

takes a lot of time and money. As a result, puppies with a bona fide pedigree come with a price. Currently the average cost of a puppy is in the vicinity of $1,500; higher prices do not signify *better*, or lower prices *less desirable*.

First Contact

Once you have identified one or more interesting breeders on your puppy list, it's a good idea to make contact by telephone or through a series of e-mails. If the chemistry between you and the breeder works, agree on a date for a visit—if possible, even before the puppies arrive. That way you will meet the mother and perhaps even see her work. In addition, there is ample time to ask the breeder various things that are important to you.

Even though Labrador Retrievers are extremely popular, the desired breeder usually is not right around the corner. But every successful breeder will want to meet you and your family personally before he decides to let you take one of his puppies. A serious breeder wants to be sure that his puppies get the living situation he has in mind for them. Generally you will not get a confirmation by telephone or e-mail.

Upbringing

In addition to inherited tendencies, good upbringing is a prerequisite for a proper start in dog life. Breeding and kennel regulations of retriever associations even provide some specific guidelines to this effect. For example, there should be no more than three litters per year, and dams should have no more than four litters in their lifetimes, and between the ages of twenty months and eight years. This keeps the profit motive from taking center stage. The nature of the area where the puppies will be reared is also regulated by the kennel clubs to prevent "back-alley" breeding.

How to Recognize a Responsible Breeder

Of course, despite all precautions, there are some irresponsible breeders, in addition to the many who do everything possible. Here's how to identify a responsible breeder:
• The run for the puppies, both inside and outside, is clean. But an occasional puddle or pile should not be criticized.
• He has only a few dogs that he keeps inside with the family, rather than in the kennel.
• Ideally he is raising just one litter, and no more than two, at a time.
• He can explain his breeding goal, show you the strengths and weaknesses of his female, and explain how he chose the sire and the results he expects from the mating.
• He can show you all the documents pertaining to the breeding and has the corresponding copies of the sire's papers.
• The female can choose freely and at any time whether she wants to be with the puppies or would rather be free to rest.

For a proper start in dog life, one prerequisite is a good upbringing with lots of experiences to test the puppy's inborn traits in combination with the environment.

A responsible breeder makes sure that his puppies have ample positive experiences with various people starting around the third week of life—but without overtaxing them.

• The female dog and her puppies are friendly and trusting, and they willingly make contact with people.

• The female and her puppies appear to be healthy and well cared for. The puppies have shiny coats, clear eyes, and clean hindquarters.

• The breeder is generally knowledgeable about Labradors and is familiar with raising and training the dogs, plus breed-specific diseases, among other things.

• He offers his puppies a stimulating place to run around with a variety of toys and things to discover.

• He provides his puppies with lots of human contact.

• He basically focuses on the puppies all day long and thus knows them well.

• He wants to get to know you as well as possible and considers it very important for you to have your Labrador x-rayed later on for hip and elbow dysplasia, and for you to have your Lab take a temperament test.

• He supports the puppy purchasers after the sale if they have questions and problems.

Many breeders also take an occasional trip to the countryside with the dog family, get the little ones used to initial, short car rides, and train them to come to a whistle. If the focus in breeding is working skills, the puppies are also introduced to water and wild game, and the breeder tests the extent to which the retrieving instinct manifests itself.

The Sire

Only rarely will you see the puppies' father at the breeder's. Usually the male does not live in the area, and it's rare for a breeder to have his own stud that is a good match for his females. A breeder also chooses different males from several litters to avoid creating a shallow gene pool. For the same reason, using the same parents for a subsequent litter is allowed only under certain conditions. But you can find out where the stud dog lives and visit him, if you have a chance.

Visits to the Breeder

Once you locate the right breeder and get confirmation to buy a puppy you can hardly wait to visit the cuddly creatures. Labrador puppies really look cute and somehow remind us of little seals.

Breeders may allow visitors to view puppies from another room but not handle them. The reason is simple: Puppies less than six or seven weeks old are quite susceptible to contagious diseases that may be transmitted by unknowing humans via their hands, clothes, or the soles of their shoes.

Your breeder will welcome you to visit and watch the litter as they develop, especially when they play together. He may introduce different toys, and you can watch a puppy that is more aggressive than its siblings. Shy puppies are noted, and the size and weights begin to change almost overnight. The breeder may "tag" a choice puppy by painting a toenail with nail polish so that you can follow it week by week.

The Formalities

Before you take your puppy home, some details must be discussed with the breeder.

The breeder will ask the following:
• Will the puppy live outside, and if so, is your backyard puppy-proof?
• Do you have a veterinarian, and have you arranged for an examination within a few days after you take your puppy home?
• Have you any other pets?
• Have you ever owned a Labrador Retriever?
• How much free time will you and/or your adult family have to train and play with the puppy?

You should ask these questions:
• Is the puppy guaranteed in writing, and if so, for how long? Under what circumstances?
• Are the terms of a guarantee written and signed by both breeder and buyer?
• Has the puppy received the necessary core vaccinations? If so, when and by whom?

• Have any booster vaccinations been administered? Are more needed? When?
• Has your puppy been checked for parasites, and if infested, when was she treated and by whom?
• If she was infested, what medication was used? Does it need to be repeated, and if so, when?
• Will microchip identification be inserted by the breeder or a veterinarian?
• Before I pay, will a veterinarian examine the puppy in the presence of breeder and buyer?
• If the puppy is male, are both testicles in place? If one or both are retained, will the breeder keep the puppy until both are descended?
• Is the puppy's bite correct?
• Does the puppy have an umbilical hernia, and if so, will the breeder pay for the surgery if it is required?
• Are you furnished the proper AKC or other registration for your puppy?
• Have you been furnished with an official pedigree?

A mother with good instincts is vitally important to the little puppies. The baby Labradors would not survive the first couple of days without her care and mother's milk.

Breeding

Seeing a litter of puppies develop with their mother from the first day of life is an exceptional and truly enriching experience. But breeding must be done responsibly, and it involves a good deal more than simply mating one's female Lab with the nice male Labrador in the neighborhood. Producing a litter of healthy, beautiful Lab puppies requires more than a modicum of knowledge. The breeder should have as much hands-on experience as possible in the art of determining the best match between sire and bitch. The conformation type, color, and use of both parents must be carefully considered; that knowledge can't be totally learned from a book. The male must be researched and his stud fee paid. The bitch often must be transported to the male if he is away from your home. These necessities preordain a great Lab litter.

Breeding Is More than Reproducing

Once a Labrador, always a Labrador— this is true for practically every person who has the good fortune to have a specimen of this wonderful breed as a companion. Thus it is understandable that many Labrador fans consider raising a litter of puppies or offering their male dog as a stud. But breeding means having a great responsibility to the breed and to the future purchasers.

There is a long row to hoe before a contented band of puppies occupies the litter basket. Strict breeding guidelines assure that only dogs that meet certain requirements are used for breeding.

Look for a breeder who follows the same or a similar breeding goal and who has dealt with the breed for a long time. The breeder must also have raised many litters.

No Rose-colored Glasses

A person's own dog is always the greatest, the sweetest, and the best—but if you want to raise puppies you have to get rid of the rose-colored glasses and take an objective look at the dog's strengths and weaknesses. Then you have to consider what your breeding goal is. It doesn't matter whether you are most interested in working qualities, appearance, or a nice family dog—you must always keep an eye on the whole Labrador package. This includes ease of training, working with the owner, plus a stable, friendly, and open disposition, and of course a willingness to retrieve. For a hunting dog breed,

this also includes not being gun-shy. You may wonder why this is important for a dog that will not be used for hunting. Even the daily routine of a family dog includes all kinds of loud noises. If they put your dog on edge, many everyday situations will be a source of stress.

The first thing to do is to make sure that your dog's health is sound. X rays and gene tests have already been mentioned. Responsible breeders do everything possible to avoid passing on undesirable characteristics and health problems that would act as a detriment to the breed. If a dog has health or temperament problems, it is better for the entire breed to sideline the dog from breeding. Despite that, your Labrador will still be the sweetest and best of all.

The Right Partner

Once you have determined that your dog is a candidate for breeding, the next step is one of the most difficult tasks in breeding: searching for an appropriate male. The better informed you are about the breed and everything it entails, the better your chances of success. It is very important that you gather lots of information about your bitch's ancestors and relatives. That way you can use the association data bank and personal conversations to find the male best suited for reasons of health, temperament, and other characteristics.

The owner of the bitch conducts the search for the stud. The owner of a stud dog is notified

that a breeder is interested in his dog. The same things apply to him as to the owner of the bitch. He needs to know his dog's background so he can tell whether the bitch is a good match for his stud. The owner of the stud dog shares the responsibility for the result. If there are reasons for the mating, and no obstacles, it's time for the trip to visit the stud.

The Right Timing

A bitch is in heat for about three weeks at a time, but she is ready for mating for only a few days. In many cases, this occurs around the fourteenth day. But there are also significant deviations before or after this time. With time you will become familiar with your dog's cycle,

and progesterone tests at the veterinarian's can also help to determine the most favorable time for mating. This allows time for planning the "mating" and keeps you from arriving much too early or too late at the stud dog's place.

If the mating is successful, the stud and bitch "tie" and stand rump to rump for a few minutes. If you are present for the mating, do not try to separate the pair; tying together is normal for all dogs. Usually a "successful" mating will produce a tie, but a tie does not produce a litter every time. Call your veterinarian for the best time to use ultrasound or to palpate the bitch after mating, usually between three or four weeks. If the breeding was successful, you should see a litter in sixty-three days.

A carefully planned mating requires lots of knowledge and commitment. But this is the only way to maximize the probability of producing healthy, typical Labrador puppies. Then you are off and running!

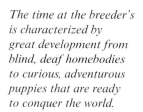

The time at the breeder's is characterized by great development from blind, deaf homebodies to curious, adventurous puppies that are ready to conquer the world.

The Puppies' Development

Once the whelping starts, there is a lot of stress. Will everything go well? Will the puppies be healthy? These and other questions go through the owner's mind. The veterinarian must be notified of the whelping duration. For new breeders, it is essential to have an experienced breeder on hand.

In the first few weeks, drinking and sleeping are the daily routine for the puppies. At the end of the second week, the eyes begin to open slowly and the puppies become increasingly active.

A female dog with good instincts rarely needs support during a normal whelping. She knows what she has to do, severs the puppies' umbilical cords, cleans off the placentas, and stimulates their circulation by licking them.

The Quiescent Phase

Puppies like to stay close to the nest. They see nothing, hear nothing, and merely creep about. And, yet, when they arrive, they need no human support. Their instinct tells them that they need to find the dam's udder; their feeling for temperature differences and their sense of smell lead them there with back-and-forth searching movements. Supposed help is counterproductive, because what's going on now is the puppies' first learning experience and their initial mastery of stress, which is very important—the puppies achieve success through their own exertions! They immediately latch onto a teat and suck fervently until at last they drop away, full and fast asleep.

Not much happens in the litter basket in the first couple of weeks; the puppies drink, sleep, deficate, urinate, and grow. Their actions signal when their dam is coming to feed and clean them. During this time, the mother has a strong tie to the nest and remains with the puppies almost constantly. This is important, for her warmth gives the puppies a sense of security. At first not even the puppies' digestion would work properly without the mother's devoted care in licking their stomachs and their hindquarters.

The Socialization Phase

Around the end of the second week, things get exciting. Gradually the eyes open, first as tiny slits, and then wider and wider. All the senses begin to function more effectively. Initial attempts at walking are now part of the program, but the puppies are still wobbly and extremely cute to watch. With physical development comes an interest in the surroundings. The puppies explore the whelping box and make the first playful contacts with their siblings. Any toys in their surroundings awaken their curiosity, and many Labrador puppies already begin carrying things around like a typical retriever. If a person approaches the litter basket, the puppies now seek to make contact. With wagging tails, they lick the person's hand or chew on it. Soon the world of the litter basket becomes too small for them, and they force their way out. If they are given the opportunity to decide when to leave their "crib," it becomes evident which ones have the courage to take an indoor excursion. The puppies quickly become more secure on their little legs, and there is a corresponding increase in the action—including boisterous group play. Now the mother is not always with the puppies, because the brood of youngsters sometimes becomes quite annoying. When she comes back, she is greeted loudly and her mammary glands get taken by storm. If her mammae are empty and a puppy won't take no for an answer, there is a scolding by the mother. The babies need their training! Around the fourth week, the breeder provides the first supplementary solid food.

Now running around indoors no longer suffices. It's time to go exploring in the yard! This too reveals something about the puppies' personalities—who explores the new world, and how it's done. For the puppies to live out their lust for adventure and strengthen their self-confidence, a structured environment with changing stimuli is important—including, for example, a compost bin, a rain barrel to walk through, or a balancing board. The puppies play with each other and with their mother and try things out. People are a real highlight for Labrador puppies, and they love playing with two-legged visitors and cuddling with them. All these experiences are vitally important to them.

What Happens Now Has a Lasting Effect

In the socialization phase, which lasts until about the age of sixteen weeks, the puppy forms its conception of the world. It is curious, adventurous, and full of energy. In this time, its readiness to learn is very pronounced—experiences and lessons learned solidify permanently in the puppy's brain. This is also true for negative and nonexistent experiences. But the effect

of the experiences and deficits also depends on the dog's basic disposition. A Labrador puppy with steady nerves will cope with an unpleasant experience or make up for a missing one more successfully than a more sensitive puppy. Lab puppies, like other young canines, naturally change as they develop, and they will remember their early experiences, whether positive or negative, all their lives.

The breeder is initially responsible for socialization. He can make sure that the puppies feel comfortable around everyday things. These include the noise of the vacuum cleaner, the telephone, kitchen appliances, the doorbell, and even the lawn mower. Another important thing in the socialization phase is sufficient positive contact with unfamiliar people, including children, even though a typical Labrador usually enjoys making contact. Once the puppy goes to a new home, further socialization is the owner's responsibility.

Get your Lab puppy familiar with her new environment in comfortable doses. Basic training can also begin at this point. When it's done right, you will really appreciate the effect of long-lasting learning during this time. You will find more information about socialization and training later in the book.

The top puppy is about three weeks old, and the little Lab below, about six weeks. Activity and mobility are not the only things that change. The physical development can also be clearly seen.

My Story

Allow me to introduce myself I am Manyoaks Bailey, Labrador.
Things are going just fine. Whenever I do something, I always do it gladly. Better yet,
everything that I do with my master is great fun for both of us!

Robert Fuchs is a committed member of a Red Cross canine rescue squad in southern Germany. Training his Labrador is a lot of fun for him, and of course for rescue dog Bailey.

My master was lucky four years ago when someone advised him to get a Labrador. The work done by Red Cross volunteers was explained at an informational evening and the tasks of dogs were presented. As an "old, honorary Red Cross person," he found exactly what he had been looking for: a meaningful activity with a dog. And he is not really the one who wanted a dog. It was his wife who wanted a "nice, clean" dog in the house. The squad leader said that a Lab was the best choice.

The two of them made a long trip to meet Katharina Schlegl-Kofler, the author of this book, who had puppies that would be ready for adoption in early August. My owners had enough time during their vacation to help me get used to my new home. I started my training after just a few days; it was fun to run to strange people (the squad people call them *victims*) and get a treat from them. Every Saturday, we went for training. I didn't have to exert myself—everything that I had to learn was interesting! I passed the companion dog test and the aptitude test with the Red Cross, and after two years I took the rescue dog test. The test was given near where I was born, so I was able to show the home crowd all the things I had learned.

The deployments around home are not too stressful. People around home are pretty careful not to get lost. The couple of times when I was on duty were just as exciting as the train-

ing sessions. And the assignments are great! You get to run through the woods and search for a human scent. Once I get it into my nose, I have to locate the missing person, and of course that's not hard for us dogs. Then I bark to indicate where the person is so that my master and the other rescuers can come and provide help. Of course there are other dog breeds on the squad. But we Labs are the favorites: We don't frighten the victims, because even our appearance is comforting.

I also have a side job: Because I get along well with children and my master is a teacher, he takes me to elementary school classes and explains to the children how to behave when they meet a dog. Once the classroom instructors have provided the students with the proper theoretical background, it is my job to go through the practical exercises with them. You have to be really calm and not frighten the children! I go up to them, they greet me, and they ask me if they can pet me. If I don't want to be touched, I simply turn away.

The children understand this very quickly and leave me alone. Who wants to be petted by everyone? My master always says that I am very easy to "read" and understand. That certainly is true. At home, I can easily communicate with my family. They understand me when I have to do my business outdoors, when I go into the hallway to rest, and when I invite my family to cuddle with me on my blanket. All

ROBERT FUCHS is the principal of an elementary school and an active member of the group Children and Dogs. He has developed a teacher's packet for teaching how to deal with dogs safely. He conducts teacher workshops and visits school classrooms with Bailey for practical training. For many years, he has been a rescue volunteer with the Red Cross, and in 2008, with his Labrador Bailey, he became a member of the rescue dog squad.

Bailey and his master, Robert Fuchs, also visit students in elementary schools. There the students also learn the proper way to give a dog a treat. As a true Labrador, Bailey really likes that!

I have to do is look at them patiently and intently. Eventually they understand what I want. One thing I have had to give up is begging for food. My family has never understood this desire, so I simply stopped doing it. Anyway, I get enough as it is!

Manyoaks Bailey

A Good Start

Your puppy has been born! Now she lies full and contented along with her siblings in the whelping box at the chosen breeder's. Certainly you are longing for the day when you can pick up the puppy and bring her home. But first you have to figure out which of the little Labrador personalities in the litter is the best choice for you. You must consider whether the four-legged companion will be a male or a female. It's best to figure all this out before the dog moves in with you. This saves time and stress. If you have other things you must take care of, do this before the puppy moves in. That way, you have more leisure when the little one is present. Once the puppy moves in, she will initially turn your life topsy-turvy. But you will see that after a couple of weeks at most, the new routine will fall into place and the little Labrador will be completely settled in. Now you have a new family member that will stick with you through thick and thin.

The Choice

Whether you want a Labrador from working or show lines is something you will have decided by the time your puppy is born. Now you have to make the specific choice of the right puppy. What will it be? A male or a female? A go-getter or a more sensitive soul? In any case, consult with the breeder.

Male or Female?

On the one hand, this is a matter of personal taste. But there are a few points that you should consider. Males generally are stronger and larger than females. However, a female from a show line certainly can be stronger than a male from a working line. Males from show lines may tip the scales at 77–88 pounds (35–40 kg), while females are around 66 pounds (30 kg). Males usually need firmer training, because they are interested in the other sex all year long.

In addition, male dogs tend to see one another as competitors, although Labradors normally are quite easygoing about this. How pronounced the male behavior is varies with individuals and depends on your firmness in training and on the dog's hormone level.

Generally speaking, bitches come into heat twice a year for about three weeks at a time, and during this time they need particular supervision to avoid undesired offspring. Group training, shows, and trials are not possible with a dog that's in heat. You should even consider your bitch's cycle when planning your vacation. Female Labradors usually are very good-natured with other dogs, but occasionally there are some stinkers. The other dogs in your surrounding area should also be part of your considerations. If several unspayed females live near your home, things could get a bit stressful with a male when the females are in heat. Also, this usually happens at different times.

Which Puppy Is It Going to Be?

Every puppy is a personality unto itself, even though at this point his or her disposition is not yet "finished." Many develop later; sexual maturity and experiences with the environment play a role. But basic tendencies are already detectable. There are gentler, sensitive souls as well as yahoo-here-I-come types that are always on the ball. Novice dog owners usually are wise to choose a puppy from the "middle ground." It takes a lot of knowledge about dog behavior and practical experience to deal with very sensitive or particularly spunky dogs. A very gentle person can quickly feel overwhelmed by an independent, self-confident, or "heavy-handed" Labrador; likewise, a sensitive puppy can feel overwhelmed by a turbulent family. Think about what type of Labrador would be the best match for you.

It can take quite a while before a puppy's basic character can be assessed more clearly, so there is not much sense in trying to choose one after just three, four, or five weeks. Of course, the parents' character traits that they pass on to the puppies also play a role. A breeder well versed in dog behavior who also takes care of the puppies individually will know a lot about his young Labradors. He will help you with your choice or suggest a particular puppy.

Puppy Tests

Many Labrador breeders have their puppies tested. Each puppy is tested individually by a stranger in an unfamiliar environment. How strong is the dog's connection to people? Does she initiate contact? Is she focused on the person, or is the environment more important to her? Does she find the strange surroundings unpleasant? How does she behave in the presence of an unfamiliar noise? Does she fetch or retrieve "prey" securely, or is she not interested? How does she react to mild stress? These and other aspects are tested. These tests should not be given too much weight; but for an experienced breeder, they round out an impression. For a new breeder, it can provide useful information on the puppies' basic tendencies. The information is helpful to the future owners with respect to dealing with the puppies and socializing them further.

It's always tough to choose, and it would be great to take home all the puppies. But make your selection based on what you expect from your dog and the one that is the best match for you.

Basic Accessories

Your new four-legged family member needs some basic accessories to feel at home. It's best to buy these at a pet shop. You can also get expert advice on various products. Here are some of the most important things for a successful start.

Leash and Collar

A nylon leash and a puppy collar are easy to take care of. The collar must be adjustable. The leash should also be adjustable for length with an additional rings and snap. That way, it's easy to attach it to a table leg, for example.

You don't yet need a retriever—or what's known as a nylon-slip leash, which is relatively thin and a lead and collar rolled into one—for the puppy. With this device, the only way to catch the dog when she is running free is to grab her by the coat. Later on, when the dog is well trained, and especially when you are working with her, this type of leash can be necessary and practical. In both hunting and in dummy sport, the Labrador works without a collar so that she can't get caught in anything. A slip leash can be taken off quickly and put into your pocket. Buy one that has a stop. This keeps it from tightening indefinitely.

How About a Harness?

A normal collar won't harm a Labrador, even as a puppy. Even a puppy needs to learn that pulling on the leash is taboo. This is not always easy to apply in everyday life. If there are situations where you can't keep your Lab from pulling on the leash, such as when you and your dog have to walk a child to kindergarten, you can use a harness. You can put on the collar when you can take a more orderly walk with a loose leash. But be careful: If the puppy spends more time

pulling on the harness than on a loose leash and collar, she will not learn very well. More on this in the next chapter.

Dog Whistle

A dog whistle is essential for retriever training. It is also helpful in the daily routine. Many breeders begin conditioning their puppies to the whistle. You should use the same whistle. You can get one from the breeder or from an online pet shop.

One of the advantages of the whistle is its distinctive tone, which is distinguishable from the flow of human conversation, plus the whistle can be heard over far greater distances than a voice. Certainly any time you have a sore throat, you will be glad you trained your dog to the whistle.

In the next chapter, you will find out how to condition your puppy to it.

Bowls

Your Labrador needs food and water bowls. Your choice is a matter of taste, but it's important that the bowls be slip-proof and easy to clean. They do not need to be adjustable for height.

Dog Bed

There are many types of beds to choose from. The important thing is for the dog bed to be easy to keep clean. It needs to be big enough so the puppy can stretch out comfortably. Many

Just a couple more weeks and the ball of fur can move in! Get everything set up in advance and do as much as possible to be ready. That will spare you and your baby Lab a lot of stress.

Remove or secure poisonous plants in the house and yard. In the house, these include amaryllis and dieffenbachia. Poisonous plants in the yard include angel's trumpet, yew, foxglove, laburnum, and autumn crocus.

puppies are really creative and work over their bed with claws and teeth. If you don't buy a luxury model now, you can be satisfied with one that won't last as long.

Dog Crate

A crate is helpful even for puppies and young dogs: It serves as a safe haven for your Lab, for example, when there is too much going on and she feels too hyper, or when children won't leave her alone. It's also useful when you cannot watch over the puppy for some time because you have to be on the phone for a while. If you need to take some time to help your child learn vocabulary words or to mop the floors, the crate is a good place for the puppy. The crate is also useful for house-training the dog at night. It's really a good idea to have a crate for the car. It keeps the dog safe, and nothing can happen even when the tailgate is open.

There are various designs, such as folding wire boxes and plastic or fabric travel crates. You should choose a size that will fit your dog when she is an adult and be large enough for her to stand and lie down comfortably. A surface area of about 2 feet by 3 feet (90 by 60 cm) should be large enough for a Labrador. The height should be around 28 inches (70 cm).

Other Preparations

The big day draws near, and you can finally pick up your puppy! There is one more thing you should do beforehand: Make your house puppy-proof.

Dangerous and forbidden areas must be made inaccessible. Block stairways with a child's gate. A pond in the yard, cellar holes, and even your favorite flower bed are best fenced off. Children's toys should be put away where the puppy can't reach them, and exposed electrical cords, cleaning agents, pesticides, and similar items must be inaccessible to your puppy. Remove poisonous plants from the house and yard or make them inaccessible.

Go through your house and yard, and put yourself in the place of your curious Labrador puppy. This will help you to deal with potential hazards.

In addition, shortly before you pick up the puppy, you should hold a family conference and discuss the rules that will apply to your new family member. It is easy to avoid promoting many annoying habits, such as begging and jumping up, when everyone works together and makes sure that the dog gets nothing from the table, and that even a cute puppy is not allowed to jump up.

*Basic accessories for a
Labrador include a dog
bed, a leash, a collar,
and a dog whistle. The
master or mistress
will need all-weather
outdoor gear.*

Your Labrador Moves In: The First Weeks

Finally, you pick up your Lab puppy at the breeder's. You go home with the new family member in your arms, and a new era begins: the time with your Labrador!

The little Labrador has finally moved in with you! This is a joyous time, but give her time to acclimate calmly and get to know her new surroundings and family.

When you pick up your puppy, don't forget the leash and collar, plus a roll of paper towels (in case she gets sick on the trip), some water, and a dog blanket.

If it's a long trip home, include some breaks. Make sure that the puppy is always on a leash during a break. If possible, two people should go to get the dog, so that one person can take care of her during the trip. It's up to you whether you place your Lab on the back seat of the car, on someone's lap, or in a crate (for example, if you have to make the trip alone). When you reach home, first take the puppy to a place where she can relieve herself. She may do so right away. Then let her look around her new home at leisure. Show her where her water bowl is. If the puppy is tired, let her sleep in peace.

It will be difficult for your friends and relatives, but during the first few days, let the puppy get to know her new caregiver and new home without interference. The young Labrador does not yet need to be walked.

The First Night

During the first night, your puppy may be restless. It is important for her to sleep near you. Sleeping alone is not natural for her; in addition, it is counterproductive to house-training if she can relieve herself in the house during the night.

As late as possible, bring your Lab outdoors one final time to relieve herself. Then put her into her crate and close the door. Since your puppy will not want to soil her sleeping area, she will become restless if she has to go out. But try to determine whether she has to go out or is simply bored. If your Lab was outdoors a short time ago, it is highly probable that she doesn't need to relieve herself. In that case, ignore her. She will calm down. Do not let her sleep in the crate in a place where you cannot hear her when she becomes restless. If the puppy has to go and you don't hear her, it is very distressing for your Lab to have to relieve herself in her sleeping place. Many puppies can make it through the night from the beginning, but many need to go out once or twice.

House-training

House-training is the first thing the puppy needs to learn. It is not difficult. Few Labradors draw attention to themselves by whining, so always keep the puppy in view. As soon as the pup starts sniffing around the floor, becomes restless, stands by the door, or walks in a circle, pick her up and carry her to her toilet area. This is also the first thing you should do in the morning. Take her outdoors regularly, especially during playtime, after waking up, and after eating. But if an accident happens inside the house, clean it up without comment and in the future keep a closer eye on your dog. Do not scold her.

Getting Used to the Leash and Collar

Don't leave your dog's collar on the dog during the day when the puppy is alone in the house. Her collar should not be too tight; there should be room for two fingers to fit under it easily. At first, many puppies keep scratching themselves, but that usually stops after a couple of days. Entice the puppy on the leash and she will surely run along with you. But run with her on the leash only a little bit and for short distances so that she does not develop a habit of pulling.

Getting Used to the Dog Crate

Your puppy may have become familiar with the crate at the breeder's. But if not, she will quickly get used to her "cave." Make it comfortable by putting in a blanket, and during the day put the crate where she is near you but in a quiet spot, such as the quiet corner of a room. This is the only bed she should have available. At night, place the crate next to your bed or very close by. If your puppy is tired, after playing or running around, for example, and has recently relieved herself, put her into her crate, preferably with something to gnaw on, and close the crate door. That way, she will keep busy and may soon fall asleep. As soon as she wakes up, open the door without elaborate greeting and preferably before she begins to get restless. Be careful not to miss this moment. If your puppy is restless before she goes to sleep, you must ignore her. Stay close by, but don't speak to her or look at her. Don't pay any attention to her regardless of how long she fusses. This is the only way the puppy will learn that fussing leads nowhere. As soon as she is quiet for a couple of minutes, open the door. Timing is important—in dog training as well as in other areas! On the one hand, the puppy must not associate its restlessness with opening the door, but on the other, you should not wait too long, for she may start up again.

Bonding with You

Labradors are very devoted, and depending on the type and line, they bond to different degrees with their new caregiver. Usually this is the person who spends the most time with the puppy and takes care of her. Cuddling together on the rug, the first little training exercises, little outdoor excursions, and feeding strengthen the bond between the Labrador pup and her master. In the process, the puppy soon learns her name when you call her. Immediately provide her with something pleasant or interesting.

Socialization

Just like human children, young dogs need to integrate into the society in which they live, in the company of both humans and other dogs. This process is known as socialization. Your breeder began this process. In the following learning-intensive weeks, it is up to you to continue it and get the puppy used to your living

Most puppies like physical contact. At first, this comes from the family members; but later on, the puppy must also have the opportunity to have positive encounters with strangers.

You can take a real half-hour walk with your Labrador when she is six months old. Longer jogs and hikes lasting several hours are permissible, but they must wait until she is at least a year old.

If you keep a Labrador in an apartment, you need to provide a toilet area in the vicinity. Initial "excursions" to this area make for a good start. Carry your puppy up and down stairs until she is about twenty weeks old.

environment and to her new one. Provide plenty of contact with different people. The puppy will gradually get to know your friends and acquaintances, and in the process various people will meet your new puppy.

But be careful—space out the contacts and keep your puppy from feeling besieged. Even though Labradors generally are very friendly toward people, they should not be overtaxed. A horde of boisterous children, for example, can be too much, even for a Labrador. As long as your puppy is part of the daily routine, she will automatically form lots of impressions, both visual and auditory. Just make sure that you never demand too much of her—for example, by putting her at the edge of a noisy, traffic-clogged street or visiting a county fair during the first few days. Show the dog a variety of venues; take her to the train station, park, or a pedestrian area. Explore the woods and fields with her. But don't plan a major undertaking for every day. The dog needs to be stimulated but not overtaxed.

How Much Exercise?
Of course you are looking forward to extended walks with your Labrador, but you need to be patient for a few months more. In the wild, canids (dog-type animals) spend the first several months near the den playing with their siblings. This is how they become fit to later accompany the older dogs on hunting trips. Your Labrador

puppy is not yet ready for long walks. Bones, joints, and connective tissue would suffer strain from overexertion. A puppy can experience strain before she becomes exhausted. Exhaustion certainly would be much too much for her! In addition, too much running can have an adverse effect on any existing predisposition to hip or elbow dysplasia. Just a few minutes at a stretch are what's called for. You should use this time for structured bonding walks. The puppy does not need long walks for the sake of exercise. Also don't let her jump into or out of the car. If she plays with other dogs, make sure the playmates are a good match in size and playing style. Otherwise, your puppy will keep getting run over by larger or heavier dogs, and even if they are playing good-naturedly, this is not good for the joints. Children often don't know when enough is enough. Make sure they don't romp too hard with the puppy.

Learning Composure
Labradors like to get in on the act and are always ready for a game, but they do not fit well into every situation. Now, when the puppy is still new, everyone wants to pay attention to her and cuddle with her. But too much of this is not good for your puppy. If she cannot get rest, she will become jittery and nervous, or else become so accustomed to activity that she demands it. This is not good for the daily routine, or for training appropriate to retrievers,

in which calm plays a major role. In addition, a puppy needs lots of sleep, and even grown Labradors sleep a lot. Make sure that your Labrador gets her rest. She cannot always be the center of attention—for example, when you are eating, working on the computer, studying with the children, receiving guests, or visiting a public place. If the puppy gets wound up at home because, for example, the children are too wild, calmly put her into her crate without scolding. The crate is not a punishment, but rather a refuge. There your dog can calm down,

relax, and disengage. If you don't have a crate, tie her to the leg of your chair with the leash and ignore her. In the absence of alternatives, she will shortly lie down and fall asleep. You can do the same thing if you visit someone or a public place with the puppy, although in these situations people really need to leave their Labs at home. Your puppy needs a chance to relieve herself and get a little exercise before you leave. Many Labrador puppies take to composure spontaneously and easily, and yet many must be taught it.

The breeder has already allowed the pups to gain some experience with their surroundings. Now it's up to you to continue using the socialization phase to good advantage. Encourage your puppy but without overtaxing her.

FREE TIME WITH THE LABRADOR

The Lab loves the close connection with his family and is adventurous. The main thing is being in on the action! This makes him a perfect companion in daily life and in free time. Whether on a hike, while jogging, or on long walks and excursions, he is always happy to be by your side. But as a dog from an active hunting breed, he loves not just exercise, but also brainwork. He will fit into family life wonderfully when he is happy and working to capacity.

Activity and Training

Careful training is an important requirement for a harmonious life together. Labradors are relatively easy to train. But there are a few things you have to do. Remember, your dog cannot train himself. He must learn to follow rules, and to obey you. The fun quickly goes out of a walk when a 66-pound (30-kg) Labrador pulls on the leash, jumps up on everyone, or thinks that every dog has to play. Firmness and a confident bearing are important so that your Labrador accepts you as the alpha leader of the pack. If you project supremacy and a natural authority, your dog will respect you. When you are dealing with him, make sure he focuses mainly on you, rather than vice versa—in spite of his "I am so sweet" look. If you invest the necessary time in his training and structure the exercises correctly, you will soon reap the rewards.

Suggested Program for Your Labrador

Not only is basic training important for daily life, but it is also required for all further training, such as dummy training. But training and activities are not some annoying obligation for people and dogs; rather, they are great fun for both. Common practice and experience encourage togetherness between you and your Labrador.

With a dog the size of a Labrador, walking steadily on a leash is essential. Otherwise your dog, with his strength, will drag you effortlessly through the city, woods, and fields.

Beginning while your dog is still a puppy will save lots of work later on. Practice every day in small units adapted to your dog's age and abilities. Training is first conducted in the absence of any distractions. As your dog develops his skills, the exercises can be solidified in the presence of distractions.

How Your Dog Learns

Labradors learn well and quickly, even when you don't practice certain things with them. That means they also easily learn things that you don't want them to. Your dog pulls on the leash, and you walk along with him. He quickly learns that it's worth it to pull. The things that your Labrador should not do must not provide any benefit. Dogs learn especially from success. It is therefore important that you convince your dog that the things he should be able to do are worth doing. But of course he should also obey you because you show him through your commanding presence that you are the boss. As a result, you should be firm if your dog does not perform an exercise that he knows how to do. Always indicate the end of an exercise so that your Lab understands that he is not the one that determines when it's over. Either another exercise follows, or you end the training session with the same signal, such as "All done."

Praise and Scolding

Eating is an absolute highlight for most Labradors. This makes it easy to reward them with a little treat. But depending on what the dog is like, your voice, running your fingers through his coat, or throwing a ball can be an appropriate reward.

A Labrador does not always do only the things that he is supposed to. In such cases, he must be corrected. How this is done depends on what your dog is like. For example, your Labrador may stand up without permission after being commanded to lie down, or he may chew on the leg of a chair. With a sensitive animal, an adequate correction may be an appropriate

Labradors are straightforward, alert, and eager to learn. Still, systematic training is an important prerequisite for living together.

glance or a grumpy *ahem!* Another dog will need a clearer message through "threatening" body language, a determined grab of the coat, or a little love tap. You must know your dog well to know how to respond.

Labradors and Other Dogs

Labradors are often strongly attracted to other dogs and want to play around, whether or not the other dog sends the appropriate signals. Are you considering attending a puppy group with your puppy? This is a good idea, especially if you are a beginning dog owner. But this type of group must have able leadership and not be a mere play group. The focus should be bonding exercises between dogs and their owners, and other exercises in which the little Labrador learns that he does not have free access to every dog. If your Labrador is allowed to romp with the other dogs in the dog school and/or at the start of the lesson, he will soon cease to pay attention to you when another dog comes around. This can become very unpleasant, because not every dog may be permitted or want to play with him. This applies not only to experiences in the dog school, but also to normal daily life, so be sure to train your dog to ignore other dogs and walk calmly past them.

Labradors and People

Labradors typically are friendly and interested in people. But just as there are some reserved individuals, more commonly in working lines, there are some that are excessively pushy and obtrusive, primarily in show lines. They tend to jump up boisterously onto every human. At 77 pounds (35 kg), this is hardly a pleasure. Keep contacts low-key right from the beginning and make sure that jumping up is not encouraged either consciously or unconsciously. If your Labrador takes no interest in strangers or is reserved, you should not force him to accept petting from strangers.

Bonding Walks

Your puppy does not yet need any walks for the sake of exercise. But after about a week of acclimation, you can include a small bonding walk (about five to fifteen minutes, depending on age) up to the age of about twenty weeks; this way the puppy will learn spontaneously to pay attention to where you are. Carry your dog or drive him to an unfamiliar and danger-free area. Put your Lab onto the ground, and attach the leash. Now start walking; he will follow you. At first, you can lure him into walking with you, but then say no more. Walk at a pace that does not force him to run, but that also gives him no time for anything but following you. If your dog tries to pass you or take off in another direction, immediately turn around and continue in the opposite direction. The puppy should not walk in front of you. Walk a bit faster if the puppy starts doing something else behind you. That

This is the way it should be! A call or a whistle from his master and the Labrador runs back with ears flying. This is no problem with the right training from the time the dog is young.

If your puppy hears "Come!" or your whistle in excessively difficult situations and does not come, the signal cannot be cemented in the desired way, and it then loses more and more significance— thereby ruining your command.

way, he learns permanently that you are gone if he does not pay attention. You can even keep doing this with an older dog in case he gets too far away from you.

Here too there are individual differences. Very tractable puppies "stick" to their owner's heels right from the beginning, but more independent dogs must first learn to focus on the person.

Coming When Called

While you prepare the food, someone else holds the puppy a distance away. The puppy will surely want to go to you. Crouch down and put the bowl on the floor right in front of you. Now say "Come!" or whistle two short blasts in a row with the dog whistle (double blast). The dog is let loose, he goes to you, gets a reward, and is allowed to eat. After a few days, call him to you in other parts of the house besides his feeding place, without someone holding the dog, and from various distances. Once this works well, move the exercise outdoors, but without any distraction and initially using short distances. Now the reward comes from the hand. If the dog comes especially quickly or in the presence of distractions, he gets more rewards. In the next few weeks, whistle or call your dog only when you are certain that he will come. If you are not sure, simply coax him with an enticing voice or his name, so you don't spoil your command in case of doubt.

Behavior on Leash

Right from the beginning, make sure that your Labrador does not pull. Practice with your young puppy, but don't walk long distances with him on the leash. Make the leash a little longer. Immediately stop shortly before the leash goes taut. Do not speak to him. Continue walking only when the leash loosens again because the puppy has come back a bit or sat down. As soon as he starts to pull again, stop. He will learn that pulling gets him nowhere.

If the puppy is already a bit older, or even an adolescent, and standing in place has no effect, you can instead turn around quickly, always just before the leash tightens, and continue walking. If your dog is not paying attention to where you are going, at some point the leash becomes taut and he must turn around. Regulate your pace so that he gets turned around, but without too much force. He will learn that it is pleasant when the leash remains loose. With appropriate firmness he will soon walk dutifully on a loose leash. Sometimes it is useful to choose between a collar and a harness. You can read more about this on page 66.

Heel

Here your dog walks close to your side and in line with your knees. Proper heeling is important in all types of dog training, plus in everyday life when you must go up or down stairs with the dog on a leash, when a jogger goes by, or

This Labrador sits attentively at heel and waits for instructions from his mistress. Then this exercise is ended by moving on to a different one, or the dog is allowed to run free.

when you are traveling around town. It really doesn't matter whether you lead your dog on the right or the left. If you choose the left, position the leashed dog on your left side. The leash hangs slightly loose, and you hold it in your right hand. You hold a treat in your left hand. Let the left arm hang down next to your body, and show the puppy the treat. As soon as he becomes interested in it, walk fairly briskly. Your dog will remain at your side and lick at the treat. As you walk, repeatedly say "Heel." After a few yards have the dog sit, and give him the treat. Take a new treat and continue onward. Also include some weaving back and forth. Gradually increase the distances. Does your puppy come along nicely? Then after starting off, bring your hand and the treat upward to your jacket pocket. Your puppy is still watching you. Then after two or three steps reward him while continuing to walk, and then have him sit. The important thing is for him to get the treat when he continues to look at you while walking. Also gradually and carefully lengthen the distances without treats. After a few weeks the treat can almost be eliminated. Also practice in various settings, including under or over fallen logs and embankments. Always adapt the degree of difficulty to your dog's learning speed.

Sit

Hold a treat over the puppy's head. Regardless of what he does, keep your hand still and closed. As soon as your dog sits, say "Sit!" and give him the treat. After a few days your puppy will also sit when he hears the command "Sit!" Now stretch things out and don't reward the dog until he sits for a longer time. Give a treat only now and then. In addition, have the puppy sit for just a couple of moments before his filled food dish, until you give the release command, and then let him eat. Practice having him sit calmly, especially for dummy work under increasing distraction, and for several minutes.

Lie Down

As soon as your puppy can sit, begin with *down*. Hold a treat right in front of his nose while he's sitting. Now move it slowly downward and straight out or slightly to one side, near your dog.

Your puppy will follow with his nose and lie down. Once the elbows and the belly touch the floor, say "Lie down" and give your Labrador his treat. Before he stands up on his own, terminate the exercise.

As soon as the dog lies down on command, he gets the treat after he remains in position and stops insisting on the food—for gradually longer and longer. Then your hand may sometimes be empty.

Stay

If your puppy sits and lies next to you calmly, he will learn by himself to stay in one place. Have your dog sit or lie by your side. Now say

"Stay!" and stand right in front of him and facing him. Remain standing in front of him for a moment and then go back to him. Praise your Lab in a calm voice, but without a treat. This intensifies his suspense, but he should wait very calmly. While remaining in place, he should sit only after your return and upon your "sit" command. As you teach your dog to stay, first increase the time, and then the distance, and increase the distractions. Here is a good exercise that is also useful for dummy training: your dog sits, and you stand facing him a few arm lengths away. Now throw a dummy or a ball at an angle behind you. That way, you can get to the dummy quicker than your dog if he makes a false start. As things progress, throw the dummy beside you, then in front of you, and then near your dog, in front of him, and finally over him as well. Your Lab always remains sitting, and you pick up the dummy.

You can also do this type of throwing exercise while your dog heels.

On the Move with a Labrador

Your Lab naturally loves going places with you. Once he is about a year old, you can take him jogging with you. Begin with short distances and a moderate pace. The same applies to hiking. Don't head for the high peaks right away. Remember to bring water and a dog snack for longer tours. You can plan some variety into walks by including some training sessions, having your Lab look for his favorite ball, or using small ditches, logs, and so forth for agility exercises.

The Right Rewards

Use fairly small, soft treats as rewards. Subtract the amount of treats from the dog's daily food ration or the Lab will soon have too much padding on his ribs. In the beginning, reward every correct performance of an exercise. Once your dog masters it, give him a treat only now and again. For exceptional performances, he can get several treats at once.

A Labrador must learn to adapt to the situation and relax if nothing is going on or nobody has any time for him. He must also stay in a particular spot on command.

Dummy Training

A typical Labrador enjoys working with his master and needs some work to exercise his brain. What could be better than providing him with the activities that he was bred to perform—fetching? You don't need to be a hunter to do this. All you need is a couple of training dummies.

Because not every Lab owner has the ability or the desire to use his or her dog for hunting, dummies came into use in Great Britain as a substitute for wild game. But they can also be used to maintain the performance level of this hunting dog during the closed season.

Dummies are little bags filled with plastic granules and shaped like a roll, with a little loop to make it easy to toss. They come in various sizes, weights, and designs. As soon as the young dog is big enough, standard 1-pound (500-g) dummies are used; they are also used in trials. Since retriever work always takes place in forest and field, training units can be integrated into every walk. They are fun all by themselves and with like-minded people. Dummies solidify obedience and the bonding between people and their dogs. Labradors are also naturally suited for other types of training. The following text uses terms that vary a bit from those used in many training books. However, the meaning of the terms used here is similar. All these exercises begin with short distances. The dummy is not far from the dog when he is sent ahead and marking, and while searching and retrieving. In a quick search, the distance between the dog and the trainer is initially kept short as well. In guiding the dog ("Go," "Back"), the distances between the dog and the trainer, and the dog and the dummy, are kept short, too. The distances are gradually increased; when guiding the dog, the distances between the dog and the dummy are increased first.

Marking

On a hunt, the shot sounds, a pheasant falls to the ground, and the dog observes (marks) it.

In dummy sport, a noise (a blank pistol, a loud yell) signals a helper to throw a dummy in a high arc onto land or into the water. The Lab sits beside the person, watches all or part of the flight path, depending on the terrain, and marks where the dummy lands. He must wait for the command to go and fetch it.

The "Blind" or Unseen Dummy

On a hunt, the Lab may not be able to see that a bird has been shot. But the dog handler knows or is told where the bird has landed. In dummy training, a dummy is set out so that it is not visible to the dog. Now the Labrador is directed to it. Directing is a special discipline for retrievers. The dog sits by the handler and is sent to fetch the dummy by means of hand signals and whistles. In the most difficult classes this can involve 150 yards (135 meters) or more, and in trackless terrain. Simpler preliminary steps involve "downed blinds." A dummy is set out where the Lab cannot see it, and a shot or a loud yell is given. If the dog has connected the noise and the dummy through marking and memory (see below), he knows that there is something out there. The blind with a shot is the last step before a true blind.

Memory—Delayed-action Retrieving

Without training, a Labrador cannot work a "blind." Memory is an important component

on the way to working with blinds. A dummy is set out for the dog in a certain place where it can be seen. The Lab is not sent out right away, but rather after a few minutes, and gradually after longer waiting times and from different locations. Advanced Labradors don't even need to watch while the dummy is being set out. The dummies are committed to memory—the dog remembers that a dummy was set out earlier, or that he has always found something in that location in the past.

Searching

There is a difference between a quick search and a free search and retrieve. In a quick search, the person knows exactly where the dummy is, such as in front of a specific bush. He directs the dog to the place and gives him a signal to search at the precise spot. The free search and retrieve is different: The dog handler knows only that there are dummies placed somewhere in a large area, such as a patch of woods 50 yards (45 meters) square. The Lab is sent into the area without specific instructions, to search independently.

Steadiness and Gunfire Tolerance

Steadiness means that the Labrador always remains alert but completely calm by the handler's side, even in the presence of numerous dummies, gunfire, or other working dogs. Gunfire tolerance means that upon hearing a gun fired, the dog is alert or has a neutral reaction, without any sign of insecurity. Both qualities are largely a matter of temperament, but they can be influenced positively or negatively by well-considered or less careful training. You can practice steadiness from the outset by getting your Labrador used to the idea that he is not meant to recover every dummy (also see page 92). Not just in training but also in daily life, make sure you don't reward restless and impatient behavior such as fussing and whining from boredom—there is power in composure. It is very important to practice not retrieving, especially with flying, "shot" dummies in marking and in driven shoots. Each of these situations is very stimulating to a passionate Labrador, but the combination of shooting and dummies often lets many Labradors "power up" further if the expectations become too high.

There are a number of regional trials that can lead to a national championship. Dogs normally progress through several stages before reaching top levels of competition.

Hardness and Love of Water

This is another quality that is expected from a typical Labrador. *Hardness* means that the dog does not hesitate to work in trackless and unpleasant terrain (such as brambles). A dog should accept all kinds of water and not hesitate to swim. These points too are largely a part of an individual dog's temperament.

The Various Commands

Various signals are required for marking, guiding to dummies hidden from sight, and searching. The individual areas are taught separately and combined only after the dog truly masters them. It doesn't matter what commands you use. The main thing is for the dog to understand them. Here are the most common ones:

• "Go": The dog learns to run ahead 100 yards (90 meters) and more from a starting position next to the handler. The visual signal is an arm pointing straight ahead at the level of the dog's head, plus a leg slightly advanced on the same side.

• "Stop": The dog stops at a fairly long whistle and turns to the handler to be sent left, right, or farther ahead.

• "Out": The dog has deviated from a straight line and is stopped so he can be directed to either side. On hearing the signal and seeing an arm held out horizontally toward left or right, he now runs in a straight line in the indicated direction.

• "Back": The dog is stopped once again in order to correct the direction. Now he must turn 180 degrees and run farther. In addition to the vocal signal, the right or left arm is held high; the dog then continues running obliquely to the left or to the right. Many handlers also use "go" for this.

• Search whistle for a small search: either many short whistles in succession or a particular whistled tune that you like. It is sounded while directing the dog as soon as he nears the dummy.

• "Search" or "high lost": This is the signal for free search and retrieve.

• Double whistle, "Come": Two short whistle blasts in succession plus the call "Come" mean that the dog is to immediately come straight back to the dog handler.

• "Retrieve" or "Fetch": These are used to send the Labrador out to markers.

All these exercises are first taught individually, and are combined only when the dog can perform them routinely.

Dummy Trials and Working Tests

In both dummy trials and working tests, there are three performance levels—Beginner, Advanced, and Open Class—where the level of the working tests is significantly higher than that of the working tests with dummies. Test regulations govern the procedure and the tasks of the working tests with dummies so that peo-

Steadiness is required even when the dummy does not instantly fly into the air and come down with a splash. The Labrador must remain sitting calmly. No problem for a dog that has gotten used to this gradually!

ple know precisely what is going to happen at a test.

By passing a beginning working test with dummies, the qualifications are met for working tests (WTs). WTs are competitions without established trial regulations. This is their main attraction.

Usually there are five stations for which the judges think up tasks based on the terrain and class. Working tests may be individual or team competitions.

There is also an unofficial "Sniffer Class" (S) for contestants who would like to sniff their way into the line of work but have not yet earned the starting authorization for the official classes.

With many working tests, there is also a senior class for dogs eight years and older.

My Story

I discovered Labradors in 1997. When I was a child, I had a miniature poodle named Vasco for more than fifteen years; but ten years later, I wanted a medium-sized, powerful, athletic dog. With these attributes in mind, I pored over the various breed books and settled on a Labrador because I liked the way it looked. That's how Umba, a chocolate male, moved in.

Kristina Trahms loves working with her dogs. The program for her two males includes dummy training and lots of hunting assignments when the season is open.

Umba showed me that you don't own a Labrador just to go for walks. He really loved retrieving and had a strong desire to hunt; but, unfortunately as a beginner, I did not recognize his potential for work. Still, we had eight great years together. In 2005, I had to have him put to sleep much too early.

Once a Labrador, always a Labrador—in the summer of 2005, I got Cooper (Manyoaks Ascot) from Germany. He and I got deep into dummy work; I attended seminars and training sessions, watched other dog handlers from time to time, and found my way with him. At first, he must have forgiven me for many mistakes, but eventually we made it to the highest class in dummy work. At the same time, I was training him for hunting. Together, we successfully completed many hunting trials. His real passion is tracking. It became clear early on that his greatest natural talent lay in this area. I didn't thoroughly understand the saying "trust your dog" until the first time I trudged behind him through the woods on the lead, tried to get my bearings, and suddenly stood face-to-face with the game. What a nose!

It takes more than one Labrador to make a Labrador, so in the winter of 2008, Tubbs (Querfeldein Azur) moved in. Two males together is inconceivable to many people, but the two of them are a real dream team. If they are separated for barely an hour, they jump wildly for joy when they get together again.

A member of the same species is and always will be a fellow member, no matter how much I try to do my best as a human. Tubbs enjoys the same training as Cooper in the areas of both dummy work and hunting.

One breed, and yet two completely different dogs in appearance, disposition, and nature. Tubbs is a real workaholic; he lives for work. He is accordingly temperamental and has a great need for exercise. Cooper, on the other hand, is a serene, confident dog who approaches life much more calmly. Both are perfectly friendly, adaptable, curious, and good-natured dogs that stay with me all day and at work. They adapt to every situation without any problem and are open to other people and animals, so they are wonderful family dogs. They are game for all kinds of free-time activities, whether hikes in the mountains or long walks on the beach. They handle long car trips without complaint and adapt to strange surroundings. Being involved means everything to them. Their consistent, happy disposition and their unfailing good mood are contagious.

Working with my Labradors is pure relaxation for me. It's really the only activity where I can let go of everything else and concentrate exclusively on the dogs and myself.

I train them all year-round with dummies, either by myself or with friends. Occasionally, we also put on working tests to see where we are in our training. Of course this also

It's really special to breed your own dogs: Cooper and Tubbs are good breeders. Cooper's first offspring are already here, and Kristina Trahms is following their development with great interest.

KRISTINA TRAHMS is the secretary of a regional committee in a retriever organization. She is also a member of the organization and has a hunting license. As an attorney specializing in dog law, she is busy with dog matters around the clock.

involves a little ambition, and I am pleased when we end up in the leading ranks. But if we don't, that's not too serious. Fall and winter are hunting season: Then my dogs are in demand for hunting tasks. Where I live, hunting is mostly for small game—ducks, pheasants, rabbits, and hares—so a Labrador is the ideal retriever once the shot is fired. Despite all the passion, my Labs are pleasant and unremarkable in everyday life; they go to the office with me and love to be around all the time. What more could you ask for in a dog?

Kristina Trahms

First Steps with the Dummy

This book provides you with the first steps on the way to dummy work. First one important point: If your dog—whether you start with a puppy or an older dog— carries or even brings things to you, this is super. It could be a toy, your cell phone, or a decayed mouse!

Carrying and fetching are in the blood of most Labradors. How you proceed with training varies according to your dog.

If your dog picks up some object, have him come to you, praise him, and calmly take the item from him. Even the most favorably disposed Labrador can quickly lose the desire if he gets scolded for fetching. Labradors like to carry things, so you must put away everything that your dog should not have. But if he sets his sights on something that's taboo, take action before he picks it up.

Dummies always get put away and are taken out only for training. Proceed slowly with training, and do not begin too early. The important thing is to create good basic obedience before you start with retrieving.

Practicing Steadiness

A dummy flying through the air is a strong stimulus for a Labrador—especially when it splashes into the water—so you should be sparing with markers in training and often pick up thrown dummies yourself. Also practice having the dog heel while you walk to a dummy on the ground, for example, or turn away from it with the dog. This applies especially to young Labradors and in cases where the dog tends to become nervous from the pure joy of working. Otherwise it's the end of steadiness. So, for example, toss a dummy into the water only rarely. With a young dog, work only over the water. In other words, place a dummy on the other side of a body of water and send your dog to it through the water. Also avoid throwing balls or sticks into the water.

But thrown dummies may "wake up" a Labrador that is difficult to motivate, or that doesn't show much interest.

How Does Your Labrador Fetch?

To approach the training correctly, you need to know what type of "fetcher" your Labrador is. Test this with a soft item, preferably with a dog toy that does not squeak. What does your dog do when he carries the toy in his mouth? Does he come to you spontaneously and present it to you pleased and proud? Great. Don't grab it right away. Praise the dog while he still has the item in his mouth, and then take the toy from

Water work is a specialty of Labradors. The dog must not shake or put down the dummy when he comes out of the water. He may shake only after giving you the item.

him calmly before he drops it. React the same way when your dog comes to you and then behaves as described. If your dog comes only to get treats, you can reward with a little morsel for fetching the item. But be careful: Don't give the treat until the dog places the item into your hand. Otherwise he will drop it too soon. He should not learn this behavior.

Does your Labrador show no interest in "prey?" Then make the item interesting. Throw or roll the dummy for some distance, or pull it over the floor with twitching movements. This often helps, but unfortunately there are also some totally unmotivated Labs.

Does your dog want to fetch his prey in safety and run away with it or take it to his bed?

You can try to place yourself so that he has to get by you. That way, you can stop the dog and praise him. But there's an even simpler way to make your Labrador fetch, and to make it appetizing to turn over the item.

The Food Dummy

If your dog brings things to your hand nicely right from the beginning, you can use a junior or a standard dummy, depending on the dog's age. If your dog has problems retrieving or giving up the prey, or if you are a beginner, you will find it easier with a food dummy. The food or snack dummy is a soft dummy that can be filled with tasty treats. First, practice indoors. Take the dog on a leash and have him watch while you fill the

dummy and talk to him excitedly. Now give the dog a couple of treats from it by hand. Close it and place the dummy onto the floor. You can also roll it or toss it a short distance, depending on how strong the stimulus needs to be to make your dog want it. As soon as the dog picks it up, have him come to you, and if necessary, pull him to you with the leash. Calmly take the dummy from your dog before he drops it, open it right away, and give your Lab a treat. If you do this a few times, your Labrador will quickly understand what you want and that it is worthwhile to place the dummy into your hand. This is a major advantage to working with the food dummy. If your Lab drops it, there is no treat. Encourage him to pick it up again, or take it away. You are over the first hurdle when the dog picks the dummy up from the floor and places it into your hand. Say "Give" or "Thank you" when you take it from him, and "Fetch" or "Retrieve" when he fetches it. Here's where basic obedience comes into play. Have your Lab sit at your side with the food dummy on the floor. Your Lab must wait for your command before going to get the dummy.

The Next Step

Your Labrador must be able to *stay* while sitting. Have your Lab sit while you walk a few steps away. He is not on a leash at this point. Crouch down and place the food dummy (or the normal dummy if your dog loves to retrieve) onto the ground right in front of you. Now whistle for him to come to you. He will come, automatically pick up the dummy, and give it to you. Once the dog performs this reliably, place the food dummy farther away from you and closer to him, until it is placed right in front of him; also increase the distance between you and your dog. That way he will bring the food dummy back to you from farther and farther away.

Go
You can begin sending your Labrador out as soon as he sits calmly at your heel. Place a bowl with a couple of treats on the floor. Your dog is sitting at heel, a few steps from the bowl, depending on his age. Lean forward and hold out your left or right arm straight in the direction of the bowl, in such a way that your dog can see your hand and the bowl at the same time. Also place your leg on the same side, slightly forward. Now wait a couple of seconds. Now comes the command, "Go"; keep your hand still! Also before starting, make sure that the dog is looking where you want him to go. When he gets near the bowl, you can use your search whistle. Once the dog eats the treats, whistle him back. Soon you can transfer the exercise outdoors. Increase the distance to the bowl, and practice in different locations. Place the bowl in some tall grass on the far side of a trail and send your Lab out from the other side

of the trail. It's more difficult if the dog has to go to the bowl from the other side at an oblique angle. At the beginning, the bowl will have to be visible from the starting point, but as your dog's skill develops, it can become visible at a familiar location only after he is on the move. Then it becomes part of your Lab's memory.

The Combination
Is "Go" working with the bowl, and does your dog retrieve to your hand? Then combine the two. The bowl is replaced with a dummy; don't forget the search whistle when your Lab gets near the dummy. If you use a food dummy, after sending the dog forward a few times, replace it with a "normal" dummy. Your dog has already learned "pick up and bring to hand," and will automatically do that even with the normal dummy. Careful: Your success will quickly be undone if you rummage in your pocket for a treat before the dog has given up the dummy. Receive it with both hands so you don't succumb to temptation.

The Stop Whistle
To direct the Labrador, you must stop him if he strays from the right direction. This is an opportunity to train the stop whistle: Look for a fairly broad path and wrap up some relatively large treats that your dog can find quickly on the path. Your dog runs a short distance ahead; you speak to him (without a command).

Like wild game, dummies must not be placed on the ground in front of the dog handler. That way a wounded bird could get away. The Labrador must place both into your hand.

Labradors are specialists in duck hunting. But training for wild game begins only after the basic obedience is in place and all the necessary activities with dummies are functioning properly.

When he comes back to you, quickly raise an arm and throw a treat over and behind him. Your dog turns around and eats it. Once you have done that a few times, your dog will stand still in anticipation of the treat as soon as you raise your arm. Every time, a treat goes flying and lands behind him. Now gradually wait for a longer time to throw the treat after he stops. Your dog may sit down spontaneously. If he stops reliably as soon as you hold up an arm, sound a fairly long whistle. Let him wait a couple of moments, and then toss the treat. Once that works, stop the dog without speaking. Gradually increase the distance. Now you won't be able to throw far enough. Bring your Lab a treat and then release him from sitting.

Out and Back

In guiding the dog to the side, and with "Back!," your dog sits facing you a couple of steps away. The dummy is placed in a straight line to the right of the dog (or slightly to one side and to the rear, but never in front of him). At first,

the dummy is just two or three steps away and clearly visible.

Since later on you will always stop your Lab to give him directions, now sound the stop whistle and simultaneously raise your right arm. After a few seconds, point your arm and body at 90 degrees to the right and give the command "Out!" He fetches the dummy. After a few days, teach the same thing with the left side. Once both sides work, place a dummy to the right and the left of the dog and send him after the one that was set out first.

With "Back!," a dummy is placed behind your dog. Here too you will use a stop whistle before sending him out. Once again raise the arm you use to send your Lab. He then will turn around to the left or the right. To send him farther out, hold the arm straight down, and when you say "Back!," raise it again. With both exercises, gradually place the dog and the dummy farther apart. When this works reliably, gradually increase the distance between you and your dog. Little by little these dummies will also become memories.

If the Labrador has the right natural inclinations and has been well trained, he becomes a reliable, passionate, and essential hunting partner for his owner.

Shows

The object in shows is to determine which Labrador in the competition is the most beautiful among the other Labradors. The judges evaluate the dogs according to the current interpretation of breed standards.

The Best Youngster is selected from among the dogs in the young-dog classes, and the Best Veteran from among the older dogs. The best male and female are also selected from the other classes. The winners from both of these are the Best of Breed (BOB) and the Best in Show (BIS). The best of the other sex is named Best of Opposite Sex (BOS).

The Various Types

Local, regional, and national dog associations conduct shows every year in many countries.

There are some shows for all breeds, and others for retrievers only. There are national and international shows for all breeds, plus national championships. The differences are reflected in the championship titles that are awarded.

Special purebred dog shows are put on by the AKC and other organizations. Some are devoted only to Labradors. Several titles are awarded at the shows. The CACIB, for example, produces candidates for the international conformation champion, and the CAC produces contenders for the national conformation title. If the dog has made it through the requisite qualifying rounds, he is awarded the corresponding title.

A Lab can become youth champion, regional champion, or national champion.

There are shows for beginners that are not judged; these are good practice for getting your dog used to shows.

At shows, the dogs are divided into several classes and by titles previously won.

What Labradors Are Required to Do

In order for the judge to evaluate your dog effectively, it is important that the Labrador be presented well and in top condition.

In the ring, the dog must trot extensively and evenly on a loose leash at your left side and stand for some time relaxed, attentive, and preferably with tail wagging. If the judge holds the dog and checks his mouth, the Lab must remain friendly and unperturbed.

Clubs offer ring training for practicing these things.

Experienced exhibitors practice having their Labs stand even while the dogs are still puppies. If your breeder attends shows, he can demonstrate for you.

What Happens in the Ring

At the start of judging, all the dogs in a class walk in a circle and the judge takes an initial look. Then each dog is evaluated in motion. You and your Lab must run a triangular or a straight-line course away from the judge and back.

Finally, you present him standing in front of you so that the judge sees him from the side. The judge inspects the dog closely and dictates the findings and the evaluation to the ring secretary—excellent, very good, good, adequate, or inadequate.

THE HEALTHY LABRADOR

Labrador Retrievers are robust animals, and because of their short coat, they are quite easy to take care of. Proper nutrition, regular grooming, and good health care can contribute to keeping your Labrador a fit, fun-loving, active dog and a companion for you for many years.

Nutrition

If you ask five Labrador owners about the proper nutrition for your dog, you will get at least six different opinions… You can already guess that there are no hard-and-fast rules about the right or wrong nutrition for a Labrador. But there is one point that applies to most representatives of the breed—Labs have a very good appetite, and by nature they love to eat. It is not easy to resist a soulful look from your dog when he is always saying, "I am starving! Give me more!" If you are not careful, you soon will have an overweight dog. A little information about feeding is therefore in order.

What Labradors Eat

If you look around in a pet shop, you will be struck by the selection of dog food brands and types, plus the assortment targeted at various specific groups. A few observations will help you make some sense of this bewildering array.

Most Labradors naturally love to eat. But don't let your dog's entreating gazes soften you up; you must try to keep him trim. This is good for his joints and metabolism.

How old is your Labrador, how active is he, does he have any food intolerances or allergies, and how much are you willing to spend? There is also the consideration of how much effort you are willing to put into feeding. It is easier to serve commercial foods than to prepare fresh meals yourself, and they are practical when you have to be on the go with your dog.

How Many Meals?

Up to the age of twelve weeks, puppies usually get four daily meals; puppies and adolescent dogs up to six months get three meals; thereaf- ter two meals are adequate, one in the morning and one in the evening.

Dry, Wet, or Fresh Food?

This question is subject to huge differences of opinion. The choice is ultimately yours. None of these types of food is better or worse across the board. The important thing is that your Lab be able to digest the food and get all the nutrients he needs. A good commercially manufactured food contains everything that your dog needs in the right formulation. Thus you should not give any trace element supplements. Check the formu- lation of the dry food. Grain should not be the first ingredient, but rather meat. Wheat in par- ticular is not a healthful ingredient in dog food. Both dry and wet (or canned) foods are available in nutritionally complete form; beef, lamb, horse- meat, chicken, or turkey may be fed raw if it is fresh and kept frozen until fed. Fresh, raw, beef knuckle bones may be fed, but not cooked bones of any kind. There are also pureed raw vegetables and minerals in powdered form. If you feed this diet you really have to make sure that the dog gets enough nutrients.

Puppies

Your breeder should give you a feeding plan for your puppy. At first, stick with the type of food that the breeder gave the dog. If it is a commer- cial food, it will almost certainly be puppy food. If you want to change to a different brand or type of food, wait a few weeks until the puppy has settled into his new home. Then gradually replace the accustomed food with the new. Puppy food is usually recommended for the first year. You will find this recommendation on the package. But, with Labradors, you can change to food for adult dogs during the second six months of life.

Grown Labradors

The energy requirement of a fully grown Lab depends on his activity. A dog that is purely a family companion, or one that is trained and kept busy in the usual ways needs a food for normal activity. Labradors that are used in many working tests have a higher energy need. So do dogs that are used extensively during the hunting season in the fall and winter, and that also work in cold waters. These Labradors need food formulated for sporting or working dogs.

Older Labradors

Older dogs are often less active. Therefore, there is special food for them that provides less energy and is easily digested. A Labrador is considered elderly starting around age eight, even though many older Labs don't look it and are in great overall shape.

Sensitive Labradors

Many Labradors have a sensitive digestive tract or allergies. There are also special foods for them, similar to a bland diet. The food contains only a few ingredients, such as turkey and rice. It's a good idea to discuss the proper composition with your veterinarian.

Overweight Labradors

Overweight dogs need low-calorie, light food to return to their normal weight. But this works only as long as the dog doesn't get a steady stream of treats from some other source.

The Right Amount

The food packaging suggests the amount to feed, but they are only general guidelines. Because Labradors can vary greatly in physique and weight and not all of them use their food in the same way, it is impossible to specify precise amounts of food. It's better to judge by how your dog looks. If you put your hand on your dog's side, you should be able to feel the ribs, but they should not show through his coat. Puppies can have a little more fat, but only a little. Obesity is harmful for both puppies and grown dogs. It places a strain on both the bones and the internal organs.

BETTER NOT!

*Not everything that a Lab wants
is good for him. Do not feed him
raw pork, spicy leftovers, or sweets,
especially chocolate. Cooked bones
are dangerous for all Labs. Fresh,
raw, beef knucklebones are okay.*

109

Care and Prevention

Many health problems can be avoided through adequate care and regular preventive health measures; others can be recognized early. Labradors don't need much care. But it can become a stressful situation if your dog refuses to be cared for, so puppies need to learn early on to let you touch them all over. This helps not only with care, but also with visits to the veterinarian and with such things as administering eye or ear drops. Practice this when the puppy is already tired. Look into his ears and check his mouth. Inspect his paws and between his toes. Look for ticks in his coat and check his eyes. You should do this a couple of times every week; then your Labrador learns to accept these procedures. Not all Labrador puppies are the same: Some enjoy being cared for right from the start, and others are impatient.

Care

Labradors are easy to care for and have no "problem areas" that require particular attention. An occasional look at the ears, eyes, teeth, and nails, and a little coat care are all a healthy dog needs. If your dog enjoys the occasional grooming, it strengthens the sense of togetherness between you and your Labrador.

Occasionally check the dog's teeth for such things as tartar. Individual dogs have a greater or lesser tendency to form tartar. Regular gnawing on rawhide chew bones, for example, can serve as a preventive measure.

Coat

A Labrador's coat is short and thick with a water-resistant insulating undercoat. It self-cleans effectively because of the water-repellent oil in the hair.

Labradors lose some hairs every day all year long. They lose a lot about twice a year when they shed, and you will find lots of it nearly everywhere. At such times, a comb is useful for brushing out loose hairs. You do not need to bathe a Labrador unless he has rolled in manure or rotten fish. Then all you need is clean water and soap—nothing more. But use a dog shampoo, because the pH of a dog's skin is differ-ent from that of humans. In addition, a healthy Labrador can go for a swim in all seasons; although, in the cold seasons, he should not lie outdoors or on the cold ground; he should be dried off or kept active. Puppies can swim in the warmer seasons.

You should go to the veterinarian if the dog scratches a lot, if you notice scabs, inflamma-tions or an irritation on the skin, or if you see black flecks (flea droppings) in the coat.

Eyes and Ears

If a bit of secretion has built up in the corners of the eyes, for example, in the morning after wak-ing up, wipe it off with a soft cloth. You should consult your veterinarian if the eyes tear signifi-cantly or if a thick, yellow secretion forms.

Occasionally clean the outer ear canal care-fully with a soft cloth and a bit of baby oil. If your Labrador frequently shakes his head, holds it at an angle, or lets one ear droop more than the other, you need to visit the veterinar-ian. You also need to visit the veterinarian if he reacts with discomfort when you touch the ear, or if you can see and smell a dark and foul-smelling coating inside the ear. Mites may be the culprit.

Teeth

When your dog is getting his permanent teeth (around four to seven months), you should occasionally check whether a puppy tooth

fails to fall out, even though the new tooth is already in place. It is necessary to extract the puppy tooth. You can keep the permanent teeth healthy by regularly giving your dog something to gnaw, such as rawhide pieces or beef ears. Do not give the dog any sweets; they can damage the teeth. Daily toothbrushing can prevent or delay the buildup of tartar.

If the dog drools excessively and shows no interest in things to chew, even though he normally likes them, the reason may be a tooth problem. Consult your veterinarian.

Paws and Nails
The paws need a little attention only in the winter. If your dog walks on salted roads, wash his paws with water. Badly cracked paws can be rubbed occasionally with salve, but not too often; that sometimes makes them more sensitive. The nails are the right length if they do not touch the floor when the dog is standing. They may need to be shortened, preferably with a nail clipper, while the dog is a puppy. Later on, clip the nails only if your Lab rarely walks on hard surfaces such as asphalt. Use a nail clipper for this, and be careful not to injure any blood vessels. These are easy to see with light-colored nails, but not with dark ones. If you don't feel confident about doing it, have the veterinarian clip the nails.

Preventive Health Care

Infectious diseases and parasites threaten your Labrador's health and are potentially dangerous to humans. But fortunately you can guard against them and thus completely avoid or drastically reduce the risk of disease.

To remove a tick, don latex gloves and with tweezers grasp the tick firmly and pull steadily until it releases. Drop the tick into a vial of alcohol.

Vaccinations

Vaccinations should be given to your Lab according to the diseases that are prevalent in your area and at the most effective time(s) of life. Core vaccines are those needed by most dogs in most areas of America. They include canine distemper (CD), infectious canine hepatitis (CAV-2), canine parvovirus (CPV), and rabies. Noncore vaccines are administered to dogs with high-risk lifestyles and include canine parainfluencza virus, *bordetellla bronchiseptica* (kennel cough), *leptospira icterohemorrhagia* (lepto), *borrellia burgdorferi* (Lyme disease), giardia, canine coronavirus, and canine dental vaccine. Leptospira vaccine may be dangerous. Ask your veterinarian if the species of leptospira in the vaccine is the same as the lepto species that occurs locally. Also ask if cross-immunity between different lepto species is a factor. Then compare the safety with the vaccination risk.

Parasites

Internal Parasites

Many new drugs for parasite control are being developed, and comprehensive information about their advantages and disadvantages may be obtained from your veterinarian.

• Roundworms or ascarids are common intestinal parasites that are most harmful to puppies. A female ascarid lays thousands of eggs that pass out of the dog's body in the stool. When a dog sniffs the stool, eggs are picked up, swallowed, and hatch into larvae that migrate in the host's body tissues. They eventually reach the lungs, are coughed up and reswallowed, and mature in the intestine.

• Hookworms are tiny bloodsucking worms that are also very harmful to puppies. Their life cycle differs somewhat from ascarids in that the eggs hatch after leaving the host's body, and larvae penetrate a puppy's tender skin.

• Tapeworms are multihost parasites that use many different animals, insects, and birds as secondary hosts. The adult tapeworm's head (scolex) attaches to the lining of the intestine. Tapeworms may reach several feet in length, and egglike reproductive structures develop within segments of the worm that break off and are passed out with the stool. Those segments are eaten by a secondary host, perhaps a flea. Secondary hosts also may include deer and other wild animals.

• Heartworms may be many inches in length, and in severe infestations they compromise the heart's action, restrict blood flow, and threaten a Lab's life. Microscopic larvae are produced by adult heartworms. Those larvae are picked up by bloodsucking mosquitoes and passed to other canine hosts when the mosquito feeds.

External Parasites

• Mites are microscopic parasites that tunnel into the host's skin and produce serum that

oozes forth and supplies nutrition to the mite colony. A skin scraping, viewed under a microscope, will reveal the species of mite that's causing the problem, and your veterinarian will prescribe therapy.

• Ticks bury their heads in the host's skin and suck blood. An engorged female may swell to grape size as she fills with blood. Most tick species have two or three hosts, and at each tick stage, they must find a different host species from which to feed.

• Fleas are quite plentiful in all American climates, except high mountainous regions and Alaska. They are probably the most difficult pest to control. A flea bites the Labrador's skin and laps up serum as it exudes from the wound. The saliva of a flea is highly allergenic, and that presents a major problem when your dog develops an allergy to the fleas' saliva. Female fleas mate and lay eggs that drop off and molt on the carpet, grass, or any other convenient place. The eggs hatch into larvae that eat about any organic matter available. After molting several times, the adults can live without a blood meal for months.

• Ear mites are nearly microscopic in size but can be seen with a hand magnifier. Ear mite infestation causes intense itching, head shaking, scratching at the ears, and even whining and crying.

Your veterinarian can diagnose and treat your Lab's parasite infection.

DISEASES, DANGERS, AND PROBLEMS

Labradors really are a hardy breed, but they still can become sick or injure themselves. Some diseases are hereditary. The risk can be minimized or totally avoided by following breeding guidelines and through responsible, carefully planned mating. Dangers in daily life can be reduced with caution, and any problems in living with your Lab usually can be solved.

Sick Dog

In general, you should consult the veterinarian any time your dog exhibits unusual behavior or appears unwell. Warning signs are frequent vomiting and/or diarrhea. Stomach cramps, refusal to eat, languor—such symptoms may point to an infection or to poisoning. Frequent urination in small amounts may be caused by a bladder infection. If the dog limps continually or frequently, it may have strained a muscle, tendon, or ligament. Other possible causes are arthritis or a foreign object in a paw. Difficulty in standing up or jumping into a car may indicate spinal problems. Dogs can't catch colds; a cough may indicate that she has a foreign object caught in her throat, or a throat or lung infection may be the cause. It's better to visit your veterinarian one time too many than one time too few!

Diseases of Labradors

Just like people, Labs can experience countless illnesses. One of the main things you will learn in this book is how to recognize illnesses that can play a particular role in Labradors' lives.

If your Labrador behaves very differently than usual, the cause may be a serious illness. In case of doubt, it's better to visit the veterinarian once too often than once too seldom.

Monorchidism

Testicular retention is hereditary, but the genetic mechanism is poorly understood. Male dogs are born with both testicles positioned in their abdomens. By thirty or forty days of age, both testicles should be descended into the puppy's scrotum. Monorchidism occurs when one testicle is retained in the dog's abdomen after the other is normally descended. Monorchid males produce sperm and are able to breed but should be neutered at or soon after puberty, because retained testicles often develop malignant tumors. Because of the hereditability of monorchidism, males with a retained testicle should *never* be used for breeding.

Cryptorchidism

Cryptorchids are males with both testicles retained in the abdomen. They are typically sterile but not impotent. They will mount and copulate with females, but usually are unable to produce offspring. Cryptorchid dogs should be neutered at or shortly after reaching puberty to prevent the development of malignant tumors later in life. Cryptorchidism is occasionally reported in Labrador males.

Canine Elbow Dysplasia (CED)

Elbow dysplasia is a problem of numerous breeds and occasionally occurs in young Labs. The upper ends of the radius and ulna (elbow) fail to unite with the lower end of the humerus. It is similar to hip dysplasia (CHD) in that both have multiple inherited causes, may develop later in life, and are manifested by arthritic changes. Like CHD, elbow dysplasia is diagnosed by x ray, and several surgical treatments are prescribed to relieve the pain of movement. Elbow dysplasia x rays are analyzed, rated, and registered by the Orthopedic Foundation for Animals (OFA).

Osteochondritis Dissecans (OCD)

OCD is another disease that is diagnosed in many large breeds, including Labradors. Predisposition for OCD occurs sporadically in, and is often hereditarily prevalent in, large dogs. This developmental disease affects joint cartilage, par-

ticularly in the shoulder and elbow, and is usually manifested by rather sudden lameness at about six months of age. It is often medicated, but definitive therapy is surgical. Conservative therapy using glucosamine plus chondroitin has shown mixed success. Surgery usually solves the pain problem for an affected Lab, but some degree of lameness remains in a significant number of dogs.

Idiopathic Epilepsy

Epilepsy is not a frequent disease of Labs but is occasionally reported. It is a convulsive disorder that is considered inherited. It may also result from injury, tumors, or possibly certain infections, but generally it must be considered genetic in origin. Unfortunately, the convulsions don't usually begin until the affected dog is sev-

eral years old, so that an inherited condition is difficult to eliminate by selective breeding.

Canine Hip Dysplasia (CHD)

This controversial disease causes hind-leg lameness in some Labradors that sometimes doesn't become apparent until the dog is several years old. CHD or a predisposition to the disorder is undoubtedly hereditary. It is prevalent to some degree in all large and in many small purebred dogs. Breeding Labs that have their hips x-rayed and have those x rays checked by experts in the OFA, and are certified clear of the disease, may (rarely) still produce dysplastic puppies. In fact, CHD may crop up in dogs from bloodlines that are certified "clear" for several generations. CHD involves the femoral head (ball) and the

If your dog limps, rest is first indicated. But if the lameness does not improve, or if it keeps coming back, the veterinarian should get to the bottom of the cause.

121

acetabulum (pelvic hip socket). As the disease develops, the acetabulum and femoral head are often malformed and don't fit together properly. In time, arthritis usually results from the condition, causing pain, inflammation, and lameness. CHD is a relative condition, and not all dysplastic dogs are equally affected. The degree of lameness depends on the amount of displacement of the acetabulum and femoral head and the degree of damage to the cartilage that has been caused by the deformity. Signs of the disease usually appear clinically by two or three years of age, but occasionally those are delayed as late as six or seven years. Signs of CHD may appear in one hind leg (unilateral) or both hind legs (bilateral), causing pain, difficulty in getting up from a lying or sitting position, and lameness when walking. It may progress to a level where the dog can't get up or walk. Those dogs are usually thin and are in pain most of the time. Treatments include hip replacement, other surgical techniques to relieve pain, acupuncture, anti-inflammatory drugs, and more recently polysulfated glycosaminoglycan (PSGAG), with or without chondroitin. That product may stimulate the repair of cartilage and is promising. None of the treatments or medications will cure the disease, and only the prudent selection of breeding stock can prevent the condition from occurring. X rays that are taken before the dog is two years of age are not conclusive. The Lab has a significant incidence of CHD, and it is recommended that all breeding stock be OFA certified clear before mating.

The AKC is now promoting DNA studies that should soon reduce the incidence of CHD in Labs and many other breeds.

Progressive Retinal Atrophy

Progressive retinal atrophy (PRA) is a serious hereditary eye disease of Labs and others, notably hunting dogs. PRA is caused by the degeneration of retinal eye cells, leaving the dog unable to see stationary objects. When that occurs, the affected dogs are not in pain, but frequently their hunting days are over. It usually causes signs of vision impairment by about five years of age. Examination of breeding stock for this disease is critically important. (Ask your veterinarian about the various certifying agencies such as the Canine Eye Registration Foundation.) A few affected dogs are treated, but a cure is unlikely. A Lab affected with PRA may lose her vision totally, but blindness isn't fatal. If the vision diminishes slowly, the Lab will adapt and live a normal life span as a pet.

Entropion

This serious but usually curable condition may develop at any age, and is not usually a threat to the life or general health of your dog. It is always hereditary, and therefore affected dogs should not be bred. Entropion consists of excess skin around the dog's eyes that causes the eye-

lids (upper or lower) to roll inward. When this condition occurs, the hair of the eyelids rubs on the dog's cornea, causing severe irritation. Secondary bacterial infection usually accompanies entropion, and the dog often squints in discomfort. It is treated by a relatively simple operation. This surgery is usually effective, although if the dog's skin is extremely loose around the eyes, a second operation may be necessary.

Bilateral Cataracts

This is apparently a dominant trait in some Labs; in one study 6 percent of those examined were positive. Bilateral cataract is the gradual lens opacity of both eyes that eventually causes blindness. Surgical therapy is possible in some cases, to some degree, but those Labs are usually unable to hunt. Just as with senile cataracts, the blind Lab can live a normal life if her owners realize the problem and do not move furniture around. Their historical sense of smell is in the Lab's favor.

Hemophilia-A (Von Willebrand's disease)

Hemophilia-A is a sex-linked recessive trait that results in prolonged bleeding and prolonged clotting time. It is caused by a deficit in a coagulation protein that is responsible for both platelet and coagulation dysfunctions. It's dangerous if the affected Lab is injured or during a routine surgical procedure. It can be diagnosed with blood tests.

Gene tests for certain hereditary diseases now make it possible to intentionally breed dogs that will not produce diseased offspring. This saves misery for both humans and dogs.

Labrador Retriever Myopathy

This inherited, degenerative disease is found in Lab puppies when they reach about three months of age. The pup demonstrates an abnormal gait and limited exercise capability. Exercise causes weakness; collapse of the forelimbs and cold weather may aggravate this disorder. Marked deficiency of muscle mass is evident by six months of age. Apparently signs do not progress after six months, and some dogs have lived as long as six years without further development of signs. Routine laboratory tests are usually within normal limits. Diagnosis is based on history and clinical signs.

Anterior Cruciate Ligament (ACL)

A ruptured ACL in an athletic dog like the Lab is a relatively common condition. Rupture of one of the two ligaments that attach the femur (thigh bone) to the tibia (shin bone) occurs when undue stress is applied to the knee joint. The anterior cruciate ligament and posterior cruciate ligament cross inside the knee joint, and those two ligaments hold the joint solidly in place. If one or both ligaments are misdirected because of abnormalities of the conformation of either or both tibia and femur, the stress is constant. If the stress becomes suddenly more than the tissues can stand, the anterior cruciate ligament is stretched or ruptured. The Lab will not use the joint, or if the dog is tough, she may try but be unable to use it. She may touch the foot to the ground part of the time and carry the leg the rest of the time. The pain must be great when the knee is flexed and straightened, but many affected Labs will continue to retrieve on three legs. This condition is reparable using several different techniques that vary in expense but "work" equally well. You need to compare prices if your Lab needs that type of surgery.

Allergies

Allergies are responsible for many undiagnosed signs, symptoms, and illnesses. No single set of signs fit single "diseases," and there are no set therapies that will "cure" them. Food or contact allergies may cause vomiting, or they may cause itching muscles or inflammatory skin lesions. Any specific allergy is rarely diagnosed without a large shot of "trial and error." And to further confuse the issue, allergies may stop at any time or a new allergy can present itself without warning.

Choosing Your Veterinarian

Nothing will enhance your enjoyment of owning a Labrador more than a good relationship with an understanding veterinarian. Up-to-date equipment and clean kennels are important, and polite assistants are a must. An animal health professional who cares about your pet and prescribes a sound preventive health care program is an asset to dog owners and their pets. A reliable, concerned professional will give you a few minutes of her or his time and will welcome your visit and your inquiries. Ask how out-of-hours emergencies are handled. If off-hours treatment is not provided and such calls are referred to an emergency care clinic, check it out as well. Look for a clinician who is frank and willing to listen to you. Try to find one who will spend time explaining procedures and one who isn't too busy to tell you why a recommendation is being made. Obtain a fee schedule or inquire about the fees that are charged for routine examinations, vaccinations, fecal exams, and worm treatment. Ask about heartworm,

flea, and tick preventive plans and their cost. The professional should realize that he or she is sharing the stewardship of a pet with you and you are on the same team. If the veterinarian resists being interviewed, look for another one. If the professional doesn't share your concern about reliable, effective, preventive care, you are in the wrong hospital. After you have acquired your Lab, check out the doctor's tableside manners. How does he or she handle pets? Is he or she in such a hurry that there is no time for small talk and a quick rub of a puppy's chin? Does she or he seem comfortable with your pet? Is your Lab comfortable with the veterinarian?

The mother dog still provides the puppy with safety and emotional security. Later on, you are the one the Labrador trusts and who provides security during an unpleasant trip to the veterinarian.

Even older Labradors want something to keep them busy. For many, retrieving is still their favorite activity. It can also be adapted easily to individual dogs.

When a Labrador Grows Old

A Labrador joins the ranks of senior citizens around the age of eight. On average, Labs will live up to thirteen years, but even older dogs are no rarity. Many don't show their age because they are physically fit. This is especially true of those that naturally are not too massive and portly, have no layer of fit on their ribs, and have always been active. But even if your senior dog sparkles with energy, you should keep an eye on her.

Changes

The clearest sign that your Labrador is growing old is the gray around her muzzle. The older the dog becomes, the more widespread the gray on the face. The paws can also turn gray. The dog's hearing and vision gradually decline, so don't be angry with her if she doesn't come immediately when called. She simply may not hear you or be able to locate you right away. Also be aware that she may become startled if she does not hear a person or another dog approaching from the rear. Now she will walk more slowly and

126

sleep longer. If you work with your Labrador, of course you don't automatically need to stop doing so. Does your Labrador still enjoy work? Then there is no reason to stop, but adjust the dummy training or the hunting work to her and fitness by shortening the training sessions and by choosing gentler ground and shorter distances for retrieving and smaller areas for searching.

Feeding

Older dogs are less active. Labradors that have, for example, done lots of working tests, experienced strenuous hunting seasons, or worked as rescue dogs slowly cut back a bit. Thus they use less energy, and this must be taken into account when feeding. There are foods with reduced amounts of fat and protein for older dogs; they are also particularly easy to digest. Also, dividing the daily ration into three or even four smaller meals instead of two agrees with many older dogs.

Age-Related Illnesses

Even dogs are not immune to age-related aches and pains. For example, your dog may suffer from arthrosis in the shoulder, toe joints, or hips. This may be the cause of lameness in older Labradors. If your dog no longer wants to jump up

into the car, or if a rear leg sometimes buckles or turns stiff, there may be back problems. In general, be careful to avoid stressing your dog too much. Not just the bones, but also the circulatory and the immune systems grow older. An older Labrador should avoid swimming in the winter or jumping over obstacles.

Internal diseases such as diabetes and cardiac insufficiency may also develop. If one or more bumps appear on the body, they usually are fatty tumors known as lipomas. This can be determined with a simple biopsy. If they remain relatively small, they simply are ignored. Unfortunately there are also various types of cancer in dogs, such as mammary, mast cell, and spleen tumors. It's not possible to make a general statement about if and how treatment will be handled. Even if it's hard to do, in case of doubt do the right thing for your Labrador and spare her some suffering.

Health Care in Old Age

Get your Lab her vaccinations, and have the veterinarian check your old-timer regularly. Is her heart still working properly? Does tartar need to be removed from her teeth? Urinalysis and urine culture and blood work will provide information on your Labrador's health.

A Labrador that has been well nourished, cared for, and kept fit with appropriate activities can remain active and full of joie de vivre for a long time.

Problems and Dangers

Even though Labs are easy to train and companionable, there still can be an occasional difficulty along the way or in daily life. Not all Labradors are the same—and neither are their masters. Many problems are easily solved, but many others require more persistence on your part. If you can't deal with them yourself, you surely can get advice from your breeder, a dog association, or a competent dog school. For questions and difficulties with training specific to retrievers, such as training with dummies or for hunting, it's a good idea to consult competent trainers in your area. They can watch you and your Labrador at work and develop appropriate training approaches tailored individually to you and your dog and provide tips.

Caution Prevents Problems

There is nothing better than discovering the world with a Lab. But as a Labrador fan, you can get into situations that you may not have imagined. The more you take training seriously, the fewer difficulties you will have with undesirable behavior.

Labradors are water lovers. But be careful— not every body of water is safe. That's why it is important that your dog be very obedient around water. Practice this regularly.

Things to Watch for Along the Way

Young Labradors in particular sometimes eat all kinds of filth. To prevent this as much as possible, you need to intervene when your dog spots the refuse but before she takes it in her mouth. Just how you do this depends on the dog. With obstinate dogs, a fright from a clattering tin can tossed near her may be the right choice. You can call a mellower dog back to you in time, or draw her attention to you with an enticing tone of voice. A grumpy "No!" may help. If your Lab comes to you when you intervene, praise her lavishly and give her a reward. If you could not react in time and the dog already has something in her mouth, coax her

over to you in a friendly manner and swap it for something tasty. Do not run after the dog: she will flee and quickly eat the junk. In extreme cases, it's a good idea to avoid areas that contain lots of trash, or else keep the Lab on a leash. As the dog grows older, this bad habit usually recedes.

Labradors love the water, but not every body of water is appropriate for them. Instill obedience so that your Labrador obeys even when she is in the water. A strong current, an absence of places to climb back onto shore, sharp objects under the surface of the water, or a thin layer of ice can be very dangerous.

Does your Labrador love fetching sticks? Careful! If your dog runs after the stick sailing through the air, it can easily get caught in her throat and injure her severely. Use a dog toy; it is far safer and more sensible.

Puberty and Sexual Maturity

Does your Labrador not hear when you call her? Does she challenge the rules? That is totally normal when the dog is going through puberty. Many dogs supposedly go through several stages of puberty, but this naturally is not the case. On the way to sexual maturity, young dogs undergo changes in their brain.

This does not necessarily mean that she forgets everything she has previously learned. But she is growing up and consequently is a little more independent. How this time plays out

Playing with sticks can be extremely dangerous for dogs. Ignore the dog if she invites you to play with a stick. It's better to use special dog toys from a pet shop.

depends in large measure on how clear and consistent your Lab's training has been so far, and what kind of dog she is. With a tractable Labrador with plenty of will to please, you may not even notice anything at all. The same applies to a less tractable dog that respects you as the superior partner thanks to your imposing presence and systematic training. But if you are merely your dog's buddy and read her every wish in her eyes, puberty will erupt in full force—especially if she is the stubborn type.

Your male Labrador is sexually mature once he starts lifting his leg to urinate, and your female Lab once she comes into heat. When this happens varies. Many Labradors are sexually mature as early as eight months, but many aren't until after their first birthday.

Rowdy Behavior

Does your dog want to play with other dogs and run them into the ground like a bulldozer? Many Labradors don't even register what the other dog is signaling. For smaller dogs, the power of a Labrador can be very dangerous; larger dogs will sometimes take a Lab to task if she becomes too obtrusive. Keep your dog focused more on you, and practice walking past other dogs without making any contact. Even if your dog doesn't do anything, you will soon have problems on your hands. The only way to combat this is through consistent obedience training and a clear message when needed.

Do not reward insecure, distrustful, or timid behavior by trying to calm your dog or console her with petting and a comforting voice. Remain relaxed and confident. That is how you give your dog a sense of security.

Labradors can be either adventurous or fairly timid and insecure. These qualities can usually be recognized even in puppies, so you can react to them properly from the time your dog is small.

Provide adequate leash control while you are out and about to channel her energy properly.

Keeping the Dog from Jumping Up

Friendliness is typical of Labradors, but too much exuberance can turn into a problem. Does your Labrador jump up and disrespectfully push herself onto every person? This too entails many problems. Start with yourself by dealing calmly with the dog and not greeting her too effusively. If your young dog or adult Labrador tries to jump up on you, say nothing, turn 180 degrees, and stand still until she stops. Alternatively, have her sit, if she is obedient, and reward her calmly for sitting quietly. If a visitor arrives, the person should completely ignore the dog until she has calmed down entirely. If that doesn't work, tie the dog away from the door before you open it for your guest. The visitor should not look at the dog. Untie her only after she has calmed down. When you are on the move with her, all you can do is call her back to you in time and keep her with you when other people pass by. Distract your dog with some treats or games.

Off-leash Mistrust and Anxiety

Around the time of adolescence many unleashed Labradors exhibit insecure, anxious, or mistrustful behavior. Dogs display mistrust by ruffling up the hair on their necks and barking at unfamiliar things or people, and perhaps also by running up to them. Usually this involves individuals who appear suddenly or who look conspicuous—with a hat, a hood, or a walker, for example— and objects such as an eye-catching barrel or something else the dog had never seen before in that location. Call your dog back to you promptly and snap on her short leash. Labradors that are rather reserved or totally unsociable with strangers should not be forced to accept their petting, although you could invite strangers to give your dog a couple of nice treats. Some sensitive dogs react timidly to visual or auditory influences. Depending on how pronounced this tendency is, gradual acclimation and distraction can help to a degree. Remain calm and avoid confirming the dog's behavior unconsciously, and calm your dog by petting her or talking to her.

The Macho

Male behavior—in other words sizing up the other dog and what it's like, behavior intended to impress, and occasional grumbling—are normal. A certain interest in female dogs is also part of this. But generally it can all be controlled with a strong leash and good obedience training. Things get complicated when a male dog's testosterone level remains too high. This type of male has an excessive interest in all female dogs, whether or not they are in heat. The dog becomes hard to control and can hardly concentrate on anything else

The littermates play untroubled at the breeder's. In her new home, the puppy must learn that she is not allowed to play with every other dog, and that not every dog wants to play with her.

when a female is in the area. He considers other males competitors, behaves provocatively, and tends to get into altercations. This quickly turns a walk into a stressful situation, and not just for the owner: The dog feels the stress too. Reassess whether you may have been a bit too permissive in obedience training, and work on it some more. Keep your Lab on leash anytime he is hard to control. Use a head halter that will control him without abuse. If he is still out of control and you're planning to show him, make an appointment with your veterinarian, discuss the problem, and make a surgical date to have him neutered. Remember, almost everywhere in America there are leash laws that hold the owner responsible for his or her dog's actions and the laws are getting more stringent. Neutering your Lab will save you money and headaches and may save your pet's life.

Labradors are happy dogs that are sociable and always want to be part of the picture. Enjoy life with them and take good care of them. They will thank you with their attention and devotion.

ACKNOWLEDGMENTS

What would a book about Labradors be like if there were no photos? This requires Labrador fans to devote time to the photo shoots and of course their four-legged leading actors. I thus thank all the Labrador owners for their contributions, especially breeders Petra Lau, Mirjam and Karl Dammer, Susanne and Reinhard Moeller, and Sabine Wolters-Arp, for their dedication. Thanks also to the breeders Princess Marie Solms-Lich, Christina Jensen-Dankowski, and Leonore Dittmer for their input.

A special thank you goes to the Labrador fans among my friends and acquaintances. Thank you to Ingrid Feitl, who had her bevy of three-week-old puppies photographed; and to Kristina Trahms, Ulrike Weber, and Robert Fuchs, who not only helped with the photo shoots but also wrote how they found their way to Labradors. Thanks also to the children of the Mespelbrunn primary school, who even came to school for the photo shoots during vacation. Many thanks also to Christina Areskough from Sweden, who kindly made the two historical photos available.

Katharina Schlegl-Kofler

Glossary

Blind A dummy that has been set out where the dog cannot see it. The dog handler knows where it is, but the dog does not.

CACIB/CAC Certificat d'Aptitude au Championnat International de Beauté/Certificat d'Aptitude au Championnat. Eligibility for the title International Beauty Champion or for a national championship title.

CACIT Certificat d'Aptitude au Championnat International de Travail. Eligibility for an international working title (e.g., Int. F.T. Ch.), awarded for trials on a real hunt.

CACT Certificat d'Aptitude au Championnat de Travail. Eligibility for a national working title for specific hunting tests.

Double Marking Two dummies are tossed one after the other, depending on the performance level, in a wide or a narrow angle. Either the judge specifies which one the dog must get first, or the dog handler can take his pick.

Drag A game animal (duck, rabbit) or a dummy is dragged along on a string for a few hundred yards (or meters) and then left. The dog is shown the start, and then works the drag alone and brings back the wild game or the dummy.

Drive Several drivers make lots of noise as they walk through a patch of woods. Dummies may also be thrown. The *line* stands in front and watches, and then there are tasks for the dogs to perform. At field trials and other hunts, the game is flushed by means of drives.

Field Trial (F. T.) An F. T. is a test during a hunt. There are various performance classes without established tasks. Which dog and when, how often, and what works depends on the judges. Several handler-dog teams are called at the same time, and they then wait in line next to one another to be sent out.

Gunfire Tolerance A Labrador is tolerant of gunfire when he reacts with interest or indifference to gunshots. It is undesirable if the dog is beside himself with anticipation when a shot is taken.

Gun Shy A dog reacts with fright to gun shots and flees the situation. With mild insecurity, the dog is sensitive to the shot. A Labrador is not gun shy if he shows interest in the shot or reacts to it with unconcern. It is also undesirable for a dog to be beside itself with anticipation of the shot.

Hard Mouth The opposite of soft mouth. A dummy or wild game is held so tightly that it is damaged. A hard mouth can reflect a natural tendency or to improper training.

Hardness The natural inclination to take on all types of terrain without special acclimation, even when it is trackless and unpleasant.

Line At least two handler-dog teams stand or walk next to one another. While one dog works, the other(s) must wait calmly.

Love of Water The natural inclination to go into the water willingly, without special training.

Marker This is a dummy thrown in such a way that, depending on the difficulty, the dog can see the flight path and the landing spot fairly well.

Memory A dummy is set out, and the dog watches. The dog is not sent out immediately to get it, but only after a while. It is also a matter of memory if the dog did not watch while the dummy was put out but knows a place from previous retrieving experience.

Mock Trial Theoretically means the same thing as *field trial* (but always with dummies instead of wild game during a hunt, and with simulated hunting situations).

Retrieving The dog picks up an item (e.g., a dummy, wild game, a toy) and delivers it to the handler's hand—even if it has not been thrown, but instead lies motionless on the ground.

Retrieving Instinct The natural inclination to pick up nearly everything that can be carried, without training, and retrieve it enthusiastically.

Show Rings Taped-off areas at shows where the dogs are shown.

Soft Mouth Game and dummies are carried in such a way that they do not fall out of the dog's mouth, and yet they remain totally undamaged by the dog's grip.

Steadiness The Labrador remains alert but sitting perfectly calmly at the person's side while other dogs are working, guns are going off, dummies are flying through the air, and so forth.

Substance Body mass determined by bone strength and corresponding character of skin and connective tissue; also frequently the result of overweight.

Walk Up A *line* moves forward slowly. The dogs must work by turns.

Will to Find The natural inclination toward thorough and exhaustive work in searching for a dummy or wild game.

Will to Please The natural inclination of Labradors to focus on their owners and to want to work together.

Working Test Dummy competition (individual and team) in various performance classes, and without preset standards for performance; usually with five stations. Starting is by number.

Index

Information

The Labrador Retriever Club, Inc. The AKC parent club of the Labrador Retriever. The Labrador Retriever Club was incorporated in 1931. Visit *www.thelabradorclub.com.*

The National Labrador Retriever Club. The NLRC was organized in 1996 as a national club for preserving and promoting the Labrador Retriever. Everyone in the Labrador community is welcome. Visit *www. nationallabradorretrieverclub. com.*

The Puget Sound Labrador Retriever Association is a not-for-profit organization dedicated to promoting the Labrador Retriever as an all-around dog. Visit *www.pslra.org.*

The United Labrador Retriever Association aims to preserve the Labrador Retriever as a working gun dog that is a delightful and obedient family companion and a sound physical specimen of its breed. The association sponsors events that allow the dogs to demonstrate these qualities. Visit *www.ulra. net/welcome.html.*

Labrador Retriever Rescue: This organization has helped find new homes for Labrador Retrievers in Maine, Massachusetts, New Hampshire, Vermont, and Rhode Island for more than twenty years. Visit *www. labrescue.com.*

For a comprehensive list of websites related to the Labrador Retriever, visit *www.labradorretriever.com/ clubwebsites.html.*

There are links to websites by region, (e.g., United States, Canada, Great Britain, and the rest of the world).

The AKC Labrador Retriever page contains the breed standard. Visit *www.akc.org/breeds/ labrador_retriever/index.cfm.*

The Golden Gate Labrador Retriever Club (*www.gglrc.org*) emphasizes enjoying the Labrador Retriever to the fullest extent possible.

The Labrador Retriever Club of Canada was formed in 1979 and recognized by the Canadian Kennel Club in 1980. Its web site (*www.labradorretrieverclub. ca/Welcome.html*) contains the breed standard, events, information on buying and rescuing a Lab, and numerous links.

Dog Registration
If you want to get a stray dog back quickly, you can register it. Here are some contacts:

Dog Registry of America (formerly the U.S. Kennel Club) offers online registration at *www.dogpapers.com.* You can also report a lost or a found dog.

The National Dog Registry (NDR; *www.nationaldogregistry. com*) was founded in 1966. NDR is the largest and most respected dog registry. NDR developed the concept of registering a pet tattoo for protection against loss and theft.

The Federal Dog Registry tracks canine diseases and helps reunite dogs and owners who have become separated. Visit *http://dogregistry.com.*

Books

Kern, Kerry. *Labrador Retrievers.* Hauppauge, NY: Barron's Educational Series, 2005.

Morgan, Diane. *The Labrador Retriever.* NJ: TFH Publications, 2005.

Morn, September. *Training Your Labrador Retriever.* Hauppauge, NY: Barron's Educational Series, 2009.

Pavia, Audrey. *Labrador Retriever Handbook.* Hauppauge, NY: Barron's Educational Series, 2000.

Thornton, Kim Campbell. *The Everything Labrador Retriever Book: A Complete Guide to Raising, Training, and Caring for Your Lab.* MA: Adams Media, 2004.

Walton, Joel, and Adamson, Eve. *Golden Retrievers for Dummies.* NY: For Dummies, 2000.

Periodicals
The Retriever Journal: *www. retrieverjournal.com/home.php*

Gun Dog Magazine: *www. gundogmag.com/tag/labrador-retriever*

Just Labs: *www.amazon.com/ Just-Labs/dp/B00007M2YC*

First edition for the United States, its territories and dependencies, and Canada published in 2013 by Barron's Educational Series, Inc.

First edition translated from the German by Eric A. Bye, M.A., C.T.

English translation © copyright 2013 by Barron's Educational Series, Inc.

Original title of the book in German is *Labrador Retriever*.

© Copyright 2012 by Gräfe und Unzer Verlag, GmbH, Munich.

All inquiries should be addressed to:
Barron's Educational Series, Inc.
250 Wireless Boulevard
Hauppauge, New York 11788
www.barronseduc.com

Library of Congress Catalog Card No. 2013001351

ISBN: 978-0-7641-6618-1

Library of Congress Cataloging-in-Publication Data
Schlegl-Kofler, Katharina.
  [Labrador retriever. English]
  Labrador retrievers / Katharina Schlegl-Kofler. — First edition for the United States, its territories and dependencies, and Canada.
    pages cm
  Includes bibliographical references and index.
  ISBN: 978-0-7641-6618-1
  I. Title.
  SF429.L3S33413 2013
636.752'7—dc23   2013001351

Printed in China

9 8 7 6 5 4 3 2 1

Photo Credits

Cover and back cover: Debra Bardowicks

All photos in the book: Debra Bardowicks with the exception of Adre: 83; DK-Images: 19-2; Fotofinder/Naturfoto online: 22; Fotofinder/Wildlife: 98–99; Getty Images: 8/9, 19–4, 26, 115, 134/135; JCHV: 48; Heiner Orth: 5, 38/39, 45–1, 45–2, 49–1, 49–2, 54, 55, 97, 102/103, 129; Private: 12, 14; Shutterstock (*www.shutterstock.com*)/ Tatiana Gass: 143

Important Notice

The information and recommendations in this book refer to normally developed dogs with good temperaments. Anyone who adopts an adult animal must consider that this dog already has been imprinted by humans and has certain habits. Before deciding to purchase a dog, you should investigate its background thoroughly. With dogs from a shelter, the employees often can provide you with information about the animal's history. With grown dogs from a breeder, the breeder should be able to provide you with all important information. Even with a well-trained and carefully supervised dog, the risk of damage to someone else's property or causing an accident cannot be ruled out. In any case, adequate insurance protection is advised.